A BIRD WATCHING GUIDE TO THE VANCOUVER AREA

BRITISH COLUMBIA

by

The Vancouver Natural History Society

CAVENDISH BOOKS, VANCOUVER

First published in Canada in 1993 by
Cavendish Books Inc.,
Unit 5, 801 West 1st Street,
North Vancouver, B.C. V7P 1A4
(604) 985-2969

Reprinted 1994

Canadian Cataloguing in Publication Data

    A Bird watching guide to the Vancouver area,
      British Columbia

        ISBN 0-929050-28-2

    1. Bird watching -- British Columbia -- Vancouver
Metropolitan Area -- Guidebooks.   2. Birds --
British Columbia -- Vancouver Metropolitan Area --
Guidebooks,   I. Vancouver Natural History Society
QL685.5.B7B57 1993   598'.0723471133   C93-091326-4

Printed in Canada

A Bird Watching Guide to the Vancouver Area

Contents

4 •

Acknowledgements

Each section of this bird watching guide was written by different members of the Vancouver Natural History Society. The authors are as follows: The Vancouver Area - Val Schaefer; Stanley Park -Wayne Weber and Brian Kautesk; Pacific Spirit Regional Park - Sue-Ellen Fast; Jericho Park - Daphne Solecki; Queen Elizabeth Park - Dale Jensen; Marpole/Blenheim Flats/ Musqueam Park - Bill Merilees; Maplewood Flats - Kevin Bell; Lighthouse Park and Ambleside Park - Danny Tyson; Ambleside Park - Tom Plath; Mount Seymour Provincial Park- Al Grass; Cypress Provincial Park - Dick Cannings; Reifel Bird Sanctuary - John Ireland and Robin Owen; Roberts Bank Jetty/Tsawwassen Ferry Terminal/Brunswick Point - Gerry Ansell; Beach Grove and Centennial Park - Allen Poynter; Boundary Bay (64-112 Streets) - Michael Price; Point Roberts (Washington) - Tom Plath; Serpentine Fen Wildlife Management Area- Jack Williams; Blackie Spit/White Rock Waterfront - Jo Ann and Hue MacKenzie; Iona Island/ Sea Island - John and Shirley Dorsey; Lulu Island West Dike - Eric Greenwood; Burnaby Lake Regional Park/Deer Lake Park- George Clulow; Minnekhada Regional Park/Addington Marsh - Christine Hanrahan; Pitt Wildlife Management Area and Vicinity - Brian Self; Golden Ears Provincial Park - Al Grass; Campbell Valley Regional Park - Mary Peet-Leslie.

The Vancouver Area Checklist was produced by Tom Plath, Wayne Weber and Dick Cannings. The Selected List of Vancouver Bird Species was chosen and described by Wayne Weber. The Bibliography of Local Publications was compiled by Al Grass.

Daphne Solecki originally suggested that the Society produce this bird watching guide. The outline of the book was designed by the Birding Section Committee of the Society, chaired by Robin Owen. Val Schaefer was responsible for compiling the submissions, editing, word processing, and co-ordinating the entire project. Editing was also done by Anne Schaefer, Robin Owen, Dick Cannings, John Ireland, Wayne Weber, Daphne Solecki, and Cathy Aitchison. Design, layout, and additional editing was done by Derek Hayes.

The site maps were drawn by Doug Kragh. The following members contributed photographs: Dick Cannings (Sanderling); Al Grass (Western Screech Owl, Golden Crowned Kinglet, Pelagic Cormorant, Western Grebe and Eastern Kingbird); John Ireland (Black-Capped Chickadee); David Morris (Barred Owl); Robin Owen (Canvasback, Cooper's Hawk with Steller's Jay, Rock Ptarmigan, Blue Grouse, Tundra Swan and Wandering Tattler); J. Page (Great Blue Heron); Osborne Shaw (Snow Geese, Common Goldeneye, Hooded Merganser, American Coot, and Brown Creeper); Crimson Starr (Long-billed Dowitcher); Edwin G. A. Willcox (Steller's Jay and Rufous Hummingbird); P. Yorke (Dunlin). Line drawings of birds were done by Allyson MacBean (teal, Sharp-tailed Sandpiper, Black-crowned Night Heron, Peregrine Falcon, wigeon and Crested Myna.) Cover photographs were taken by Al Grass (birdwatchers); Edwin G. A. Willcox (Evening Grosbeak and Song Sparrow); Sharon Toochin (Arctic Tern).

The Vancouver area is one of the most spectacular places to observe birds in North America. It contains a vast array of habitat types - mountains, forests, bogs, freshwater lakes and streams, marine inlets and bays, freshwater and brackish marshes, mudflats, and rocky shorelines. Over 250 species of birds can be seen here on an annual basis, and over 360 have been seen at least once.

In addition to providing birding opportunities through a diversity of habitat types, the Fraser River Estuary is also a major stopping point for birds along the Pacific Flyway. Millions of shorebirds and waterfowl pass through here on their migratory routes between Siberia, Alaska, and northern Canada, and Texas, Central America, and South America. The area is also a major wintering spot for raptors (large predatory birds).

The Ecology of Greater Vancouver

Greater Vancouver's natural environment encompasses four large systems.

1.   Along the mountainous North Shore is a large forest association of western hemlock, western red cedar, and Douglas fir, which extends for 50 km (31 mi) between Georgia Strait and Pitt Lake. This area is full of ravines and canyons, with three large freshwater lakes (Capilano, Seymour, and Coquitlam), which provide Vancouver area residents with their drinking water.

2.   Along the shoreline is the coastal/intertidal area, rich in marine life. Brackish marshes are found at Roberts Bank and Sturgeon Bank to the west of Richmond and Delta. Mudflats are found at Boundary Bay and Semiahmoo Bay to the south, and at Maplewood and Port Moody in Burrard Inlet to the north. Rocky shorelines occur along most of Burrard Inlet and Indian Arm.

3.   The major freshwater environment is represented by the Fraser River Systems. The Fraser River itself has two arms going through Greater Vancouver. The more southern Middle Arm is the larger of the two and carries 80% of the water flow. Other major freshwater bodies associated with the Fraser River are: a) the Brunette River system in Burnaby and New Westminster (which includes Burnaby and Deer Lakes), b) Pitt Lake and the Pitt River in Port Coquitlam and Pitt Meadows, c) the Coquitlam River in Coquitlam, d) the Salmon River around Coquitlam, Langley, Fort Langley, and Surrey.

4.   The Fraser Lowland Systems include numerous creeks and the Campbell, Serpentine, and Nicomekl Rivers with their floodplains in Surrey and Delta. Along with the Fraser River they all form the Fraser River Delta which covers 590 square km (212 square mi), the largest of the deltas on Canada's Pacific coast. Burns Bog in Delta and North Sea Island and Iona Island in Richmond are included here.

6 · *The Vancouver Area*

The bird life in the Vancouver area is changing because of population growth. About 1.7 million people now live in the Lower Fraser River Basin, which is more than half of the population of British Columbia. About 600,000 more people are expected to live here in the next 20 years. The region is undergoing rapid population growth. Urban sprawl and farming have resulted in considerable habitat loss. The diking of wetlands is a major concern. Some 70% of the original freshwater marshes and 90% of the saltwater and brackish marshes have been lost over the last 100 years.

There has also been an impact on bird life through the introduction and expansion of alien species. The *European Starling* first appeared in B.C. about 45 years ago. Now flocks of thousands of these birds are common around Vancouver. The *European Starling* displaces many local hole-nesting species such as *Purple Martin, Lewis' Woodpecker,* and *Western Bluebird*, and is thought to be responsible for the decline in populations of the *Crested Myna,* also an alien species. Other invasions which have an impact on bird life are from predators such as the gray squirrel and Virginia opossum.

Many parks and sanctuaries have been created in an effort to preserve and encourage bird life. The Greater Vancouver Regional District Parks system contains 10,000 ha ((24,700 ac) of valuable bird habitat. There are many municipal parks as well, including the well known Stanley Park at Vancouver's West End. Wildlife refuges include Reifel and Alaksen in Delta, and Addington Marsh in Pitt Meadows.

With its diverse habitat types and its important role in migration, the Vancouver area is an exciting place to watch birds at all times of the year. There are unique species such as the *Crested Myna,* and unique concentrations of other species such as shorebirds, waterfowl, and raptors. Persistent birders will be rewarded.

How to Use This Book

The 24 locations described here are grouped by general locations in the Vancouver area. A wide range of habitat types is represented.

Each section contains a description of how to get to the site from major roads. In some cases bus routes are also given. A site map is provided to make it easier to locate the features referred to in the site descriptions.

Descriptions for each location contain an overview of the major species of interest to be found there - either unique species, or species with large populations. This will enable the birder to prepare field identification skills for certain species before visiting the site.

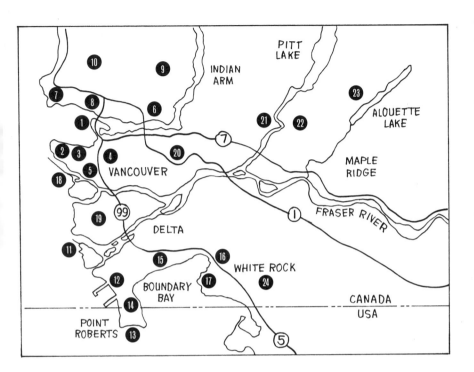

The Vancouver Area
(Numbers refer to Locations listed in Contents, p. 3

The areas described in the book are favourite birding spots for members of the Vancouver Natural History Society. The Society conducts about 150 field trips annually, and you are invited to attend one as an introduction to bird watching in the Vancouver area. Information about field trips is contained in the Society's quarterly magazine *DISCOVERY*. This is available for sale at the Vancouver Public Aquarium gift shop (The Clamshell). Otherwise, information can be obtained through the Society's "Events Line" at (604) 738-3177.

The Vancouver Natural History Society also operates a "Rare Bird Alert". If you are interested in knowing the unusual birding opportunities on a particular day call the Alert at (604) 737-9910. We welcome your comments. Please contact the Society at P.O. Box 3021, Vancouver, B.C. V6B 3X5.

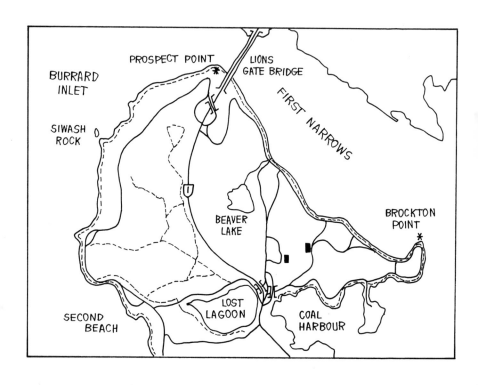

Stanley Park

Stanley Park is a peninsula of beautiful forests, gardens, freshwater lakes, and shorelines next to Vancouver's densely populated West End. With more than 230 species of birds reliably reported from the park, and new ones added every year, it has been a favourite birding area of Vancouverites for generations.

DIRECTIONS

To reach Stanley Park from downtown Vancouver, drive west on Georgia Street and turn right just opposite Lost Lagoon, or head north along English Bay on Beach Avenue. The drive which encircles the park is one-way counter-clockwise. From North Vancouver or West Vancouver, drive south across the Lions Gate Bridge (Highway 99) and turn right immediately after entering the park. This exit joins the park drive near Prospect Point, but is closed in morning rush hours to discourage commuter traffic. By bus from Vancouver, take the #11 Stanley Park bus which stops at the park entrance beside Lost Lagoon. In the summer, there is bus service around the park drive with stops at major attractions.

BIRD SPECIES

Winter

Lost Lagoon is perhaps the most familiar birding spot in Stanley Park. From late September to early May, the lagoon teems with waterbirds. These are mainly diving ducks, but there are also hundreds of *Canada Geese, Mallard,* and *American Coot,* and smaller numbers of other species. The commonest diving ducks are *Greater Scaup, Lesser Scaup, Common Goldeneye,* and *Barrow's Goldeneye.* Most of the *goldeneyes* use the lagoon as a night-time roost, departing at dawn and returning in late afternoon. The *Lesser Scaup* seem to do the opposite, apparently feeding elsewhere at night and sleeping in the lagoon during the day. Lost Lagoon is an excellent place to learn to tell *Greater Scaup* from *Lesser Scaup.*

Park visitors enjoy feeding the ducks and geese. Large grain-filled feeders supplied by the Parks Board are meant mainly for the park's wing-clipped *Mute Swans,* but the ducks and geese manage to get a large share. Thirty or 40 *Canvasback* are usually present, and this is one of few places where wild *Canvasback* can be seen as close as 3-4 m (10-13 ft).

Lost Lagoon is the best place near Vancouver to find *Ring-necked Duck* or *Redhead.* One or two can usually be found among the diving ducks. Occasionally, an even rarer duck shows up. The first *Tufted Duck* ever seen in Canada was sighted here in 1961, and one of these rare Old-World ducks has been present for part of the winter at least every other year since then. A male *Smew* - a small Old-World merganser - was present for a week in November 1970. This was the first of only three records for B.C.

Do not miss the stone bridge that crosses the creek just west of Lost Lagoon: it is a great spot for winter birding. The tangle of shrubbery just east of the bridge contains several feeders which are usually hopping with **Dark-eyed Juncos, Song and Fox Sparrows, Rufous-sided Towhees, Black-capped Chickadees, Red-winged Blackbird,** and an occasional **Golden-crowned Sparrow** or **Brown-headed Cowbird**. Closer inspection of the shrubbery will usually reveal more birds, possibly the **Virginia Rail** that has been known to winter here. Many **Wood Duck** and a few escaped **Mandarin Duck** can be seen in the stream.

The coniferous forests which cover much of Stanley Park are often very quiet in winter. You may walk for more than a kilometre without seeing a bird, then suddenly find yourself surrounded by a feeding flock of mixed-species. These flocks usually include **Golden-crowned and Ruby-crowned Kinglets, Black-capped and Chestnut-backed Chickadees**, a **Brown Creeper** or two, and often a **Red-breasted Nuthatch** or a **Downy or Hairy Woodpecker.** The frantic activity lasts a few moments, then all is silent again. Along the often dank and dripping trails, you may be lucky enough to spot a **Red-breasted Sapsucker** or a **Northern Goshawk**, but there are generally more landbirds around the alder stands and ornamental plantings than in the conifer forest. Some erratically supplied bird feeders near Second Beach, Lost Lagoon, and Coal Harbour often allow close looks at normally-shy forest birds like the **Chestnut-backed Chickadee**. Sometimes they will even eat from your hand.

A walk along the Stanley Park seawall allows you to see impressive numbers of diving ducks, especially **Surf Scoter** and **Barrow's Goldeneye.** Vancouver has the largest known winter concentrations of **Barrow's Goldeneye** in the world, as documented by the Vancouver Natural History Society's Christmas Bird Counts. A raft of 4000 or more **Western Grebe** usually winters in English Bay off Ferguson Point. Other common winter waterbirds include **Red-throated and Common Loons, Horned and Red-necked Grebes, Double-crested and Pelagic Cormorants, American Wigeon, Greater Scaup, Oldsquaw, Black Scoter, Common Goldeneye, Bufflehead, Red-breasted Merganser, Glaucous-winged, Mew,** and **Thayer's Gulls, Pigeon Guillemot** and **Marbled Murrele**t. Other species are more localized. The **Harlequin Duck** is likely to be sighted off of Ferguson Point and **Brandt's Cormorant** may be seen on the Burnaby Shoal marker off Brockton Point. At low tide, **Black Turnstone** and **Sanderling** can often be seen on the rocks near Ferguson Point, and a **Eurasian Wigeon** can sometimes be found with the **American Wigeon.** During at least four winters, a **King Eider** has accompanied the flocks of **Surf Scoters**.

Spring

Spring migration extends from late February, when most of the **American Robin** population arrives, to the first week of June when a few straggling **Western Wood-Pewees, Western Tanagers,** and **Wilson's Warblers** may still be passing through.

However, the peak occurs in late April and early May, when the park may be almost choked with birds some days. The commonest species are **White-crowned and Golden-crowned Sparrow, Yellow-rumped and Wilson's Warbler**, which may exceed 100 in a day. Look for migrating songbirds along forest edges and ornamental plantings, for example the Lost Lagoon pitch and putt course. You can also see them in forested areas , especially among stands of flowering broadleaf maple trees near Brockton Point and Third Beach. Broadleaf maple flowers, which reach their peak in late April, offer a ready supply of insects for the hungry warblers.

Canvasback (male)

Other species of landbirds which migrate regularly through Stanley Park include: **Vaux's Swift, Rufous Hummingbird, Western Wood-Pewee, Tree Swallow, Ruby-crowned Kinglet, Townsend's Solitaire, Hermit Thrush, Varied Thrush, American Pipit, Solitary and Warbling Vireo, Orange-crowned, Nashville, Yellow, Black-throated Gray, and Townsend's Warbler, Western Tanager,** and **Savannah and Lincoln's Sparrow.** Some of these species breed in the park, and most of them are found in both spring and fall, but a few such as **Townsend's Solitaire** and **Nashville Warbler**, are seen almost exclusively in spring.

Waterbird migration in Stanley Park is not as spectacular as it is on the Fraser delta, but you are more likely to see unusual species like *Yellow-billed Loon, Eurasian Wigeon,* and *Tufted Duck.* They are more likely seen in spring than in midwinter.

Summer

Some species, such as the *Bald Eagle,* begin breeding as early as late February, but most breeding activity takes place from late May through July. The nesting seabird colony on the Prospect Point cliffs, just west of the Lions Gate Bridge, includes about 60 to 70 pairs of *Pelagic Cormorants,* and a dozen or so pairs of *Glaucous-winged Gulls* and *Pigeon Guillemots.* A few pairs of gulls usually nest on the concrete bases of the Lions Gate Bridge towers, and a few gulls and cormorants try to nest on Siwash Rock. You can see the colony best from the seawall walk at its base, or with a telescope from Ambleside Park, just across Burrard Inlet.

Be sure to see the *Great Blue Heron* colony in several large western red cedars located between the Zoo and Malkin Bowl. It is one of the few heronries in B.C. located in such a heavily-used area. You can watch the herons' activities without fear of disturbing them. There is an interpretative display and viewing area set up in the zoo grounds.

Great Blue Herons are not the only large birds to nest in Stanley Park. A pair of *Bald Eagles* has recently occupied a nest at an easily-observed location just east of Beaver Lake and north of the miniature railway. *Canada Goose, Wood Duck* (which use nest-boxes near Beaver Lake) and *Mallard* are the dominant breeding waterfowl in the park. In addition to the nesting geese, as many as 1,500 non-breeding or post-breeding geese find safety in the park from late June and to early July during their brief flightless period, when they moult their wing-feathers. For the last few years, wildlife agencies and park staff have staged a "goose roundup" to counteract the effects of this temporary population explosion. The flightless geese are herded into the Lost Lagoon tennis courts, transferred to turkey trucks, and distributed to areas of the Lower Mainland where they will not be a problem.

In June and July, the Beaver Lake area is the best part of the park to see a large variety of birds, partly because its denser forest stands support species such as *Hammond's Flycatcher* and *Townsend's Warbler.* You may also find *Hairy Woodpecker, Olive-sided* and *Western Flycatchers, Red-breasted Nuthatch, Brown Creeper, Golden-crowned Kinglet, Solitary Vireo, Orange-crowned, Black-throated Gray,* and *Wilson's Warblers, Western Tanager,* and *Black-headed Grosbeak.* In the shrubbery around the lake look for breeding *Willow Flycatchers, Yellow Warbler, Song Sparrows,* and *Red-winged Blackbird.* The lily-choked lake itself has breeding *Wood Duck, Mallard,* and, in some years, *Pied-billed Grebe.*

Fall

The Fall migration of landbirds takes place mainly between mid-August and mid-October. Concentrations tend to be smaller than those in spring, in part because of the more stable fall weather. Most of the common landbird species in fall are the same as those listed for spring, but you have a better chance of seeing an out-of-range vagrant, perhaps because of the high percentage of inexperienced juvenile birds. Unusual passerine species seen in fall include *Say's Phoebe, Ash-throated Flycatcher, Clark's Nutcracker, Philadelphia Vireo, Palm Warbler, Black-and-white Warbler, American Redstart, Northern Waterthrush, Grasshopper Sparrow,* and *Rusty Blackbird.*

During August migrating shorebirds begin to appear. Repeated visits to Ferguson Point and upper Coal Harbour low tide, preferably before 10:00 a.m., may allow you to see *Greater and Lesser Yellowlegs, Least and Western Sandpipers*, and *Black-bellied Plover*, and possibly a *Wandering Tattler* or a *phalarope.*

The most interesting time to go birdwatching is on a cold, clear day with brisk northwest winds following several overcast rainy days. Such weather triggers southward movements of many species, from ducks and birds of prey to sparrows. Northwest winds are especially favourable for observing southward-flying raptors. There is a fall migration route along the North Shore Mountains, and some of these birds cross over into Vancouver via the First Narrows. Among the commoner species like *Red-tailed Hawk, Sharp-shinned Hawk*, and *Cooper's Hawk*, you may be lucky enough to spot a *Turkey Vulture* or an *Osprey*. On a cold-front day in late September, you may also find large numbers of *Yellow-rumped Warbler, American Pipit, Savannah Sparrow, Dark-eyed Junco,* and *Ruby-crowned Kinglet,* as well as late-departing individuals of several other warbler species. After a cold front in mid-October, you may find dozens of *Bufflehead*, a *Ring-necked Duck*, or a small flock of *Hooded Merganser* on Lost Lagoon where there were none the day before.

Along English Bay and Burrard Inlet look for unusual gulls and terns. Large flocks of *Bonaparte's Gull* feed offshore from August through December. They are often joined from August through late October by *Common Tern,* which, unlike the *Bonaparte's Gulls,* are not seen in the spring. Small numbers of *Franklin's Gull* are seen regularly with the *Bonaparte's Gull,* and rarer species like the *Heermann's and Sabine's Gulls* and *Caspian, Arctic, and Forster's Terns* have been recorded. In September and October, *Parasitic Jaeger* are regularly seen off Siwash Rock and Ferguson Point, harassing gulls and terns in an effort to steal fish from them. A scan of English Bay may reveal a *Rhinoceros Auklet* among the much commoner *Marbled Murrelet* and *Pigeon Guillemot.*

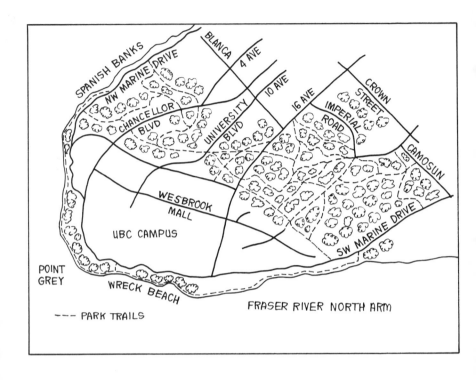

Pacific Spirit Regional Park and UBC Campus

Most of this Greater Vancouver Regional District park is forest, including some of the oldest and most diverse second growth stands in the Lower Mainland. The forest spreads across a gently rounded, undulating plateau bounded by steep cliffs and gullies with beaches and marsh below.

In the early 1860s the tip of the Point Grey peninsula was reserved from settlement to defend the Crown Colony from potential American or Russian invaders. The first timber leases were granted in 1865; the entire park has since been logged, much of it selectively. In 1923 the area became an endowment to the future university and several subdivisions were carved out of the forest. Some later subdivision attempts were halted after the land was cleared. The vegetation has since grown back into thick red alder and cottonwood stands.

As the city surrounded the remaining woods, the forest became more popular for naturalists, horseback riders and walkers. Today the area is protected within Pacific Spirit Regional Park and contains many different vegetation associations from abandoned pasture land to mature evergreen forest, beaches and bogs. The diversity of habitats supports numerous bird species.

DIRECTIONS

Pacific Spirit Regional Park stretches across the tip of the Point Grey Peninsula, just north of the mouth of the Fraser River and west of Vancouver's downtown core. Formerly known as the University Endowment Lands, the park surrounds the University of British Columbia and is easy to reach by car or city bus along 4th Avenue, 10th Avenue, 16th Avenue, or SW Marine Drive. Over 50 km of trails lead through a mosaic of good birding habitats within minutes of downtown Vancouver.

BIRD SPECIES

Follow Marine Drive all the way around the point. From Spanish Banks past the campus and east again to Camosun Street look for Bald Eagles perched on cedar snags. Several other roads cut through the park, and many more trail heads await exploration at the ends of neighbourhood streets.

Start your hike at the Pacific Spirit Park Centre where maps, washrooms and parking are available. Other good places to start are from Imperial Road at the hairpin turn, or any one of several trails where they cross major roads.

Coniferous Forest

The famous west coast evergreens flourish in the large area south of 16th Avenue, where the dense canopy dominated by Douglas fir rustles with bird life. You may get tired from peering up into the dark branches, but patience may pay off with good observations of **Brown Creeper, Golden-crowned Kinglet** and other often unseen species going about their business oblivious to your presence. The movements of hunting owls may also catch your eye as they search the open forest floor in the deep shade. **Northern Saw-whet, Barred, Western Screech** and **Great-horned Owls** are known to nest in the park, and others have been sighted.

The power line along Imperial Trail cuts a welcome swath through the canopy and the sunlit salmonberry layer beneath the lines is often busy with bird life. Salmonberry begins to bloom in early April some years. As soon as the large magenta blossoms appear, you may hear the buzz of foraging male **Rufous Hummingbird**. Later as the air warms and the females arrive, watch for their bright courtship flights against the evergreen backdrop. This power line and others in the park are also good places to spot hunting owls at dusk, particularly in early fall.

As you wander south of Imperial Trail, farther from the spine of the peninsula, more moisture in the soil allows for more western hemlock, western red cedar, and Sitka spruce to grow, resulting in a more diverse rain forest with a thicker deciduous understory. **Purple Finch, Winter Wren,** and **Western Flycatcher** abound. Where large trees have fallen, listen for the song of the **Black-throated Gray Warbler** in spring. In the more mixed areas of the forest **Hutton's Vireo** sings in the clearings.

Deciduous Forest

North of 16th Avenue, patches of coniferous and mixed forest can be found, but most of the area has been recently disturbed. Large stands of even-aged red alder are interrupted by sunny patches of bitter cherry and fragrant black cottonwood, while the ravines and steep slopes at the northern edge are full of broadleaf maple. Edges of subdivisions, ravines and clearings provide the best birding spots.

The old pasture clearing called the Plains of Abraham at the north end of Pioneer Trail is a sun trap on spring mornings and a berry feast in the fall, and is often busy with many species of songbirds. Start from the trailhead kiosk on northwest Marine Drive just west of the most western concession stand at Spanish Banks, where washrooms and parking are available.

Ocean Beach

The rocky beaches west of sandy Spanish Banks are one of the best places in the Vancouver area to view sea ducks. All three **scoter** species can be seen here from October to April, as well as **Barrow's Goldeneye**. . Watch for shorebirds too, including **Black Oystercatcher.** Be sure to walk as far as the old searchlight towers, and check the breakwater at Wreck Beach for accidental species blown in from the sea. The city can seem very far away from this wild landscape of wind, waves, and towering cliffs.

Start from the Acadia trailhead at the park entrance sign on northwest Marine Drive, where washrooms and parking are available, or hike down one of the steep trails to Wreck Beach from the campus. Be forewarned that most of the waterfront in the park has clothing-optional status, and sunbathers in a natural state can be encountered on any mild or sunny day.

Booming Grounds Marsh

The Wreck Beach breakwater protects the estuarine marsh to the south. Here fresh water from the Fraser River's North Arm collects and logs are stored. The trail follows the base of the steep slope past secluded sunbathing areas. The *Marsh Wren* and other marsh species rustle among the cattails, and *Virginia Rail* winters in the marshes near the mouth of Booming Grounds Creek close to the park boundary. Various duck and shorebird species can also be found in this increasingly rare habitat. Walk south from the busy beach area, or hike down from the historic monument parking lot on Marine Drive to the quieter marsh area below.

Western Screech - Owl

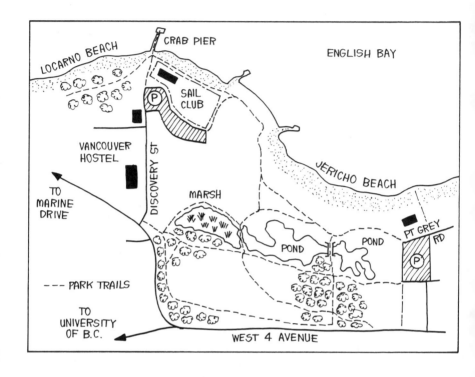

Jericho Park, Jericho Beach and English Bay

JERICHO PARK

Situated on English Bay close to the University of British Columbia, Jericho is probably one of the best city parks for birding. At 54 ha (130 ac) the park is less than one sixth the area of Stanley Park, yet it can offer almost the same number of species. Many unusual and accidental species have been found here.

The park has had a chequered history. The name derives from Jerry's Cove, after one Jeremiah Rogers who in the 1860s established a base camp on the edge of the wilderness and set about felling the enormous trees that once grew here. A few stumps from this era can be found in the park. Later, picnickers came by barge from downtown Vancouver. The area then became part of a golf course for the Jericho Country Club. In 1942, the Federal Department of National Defence bought most of the land and built an airstrip, remains of which are seen in the large concrete wharf east of the Sailing Club. In 1973, the land was sold back to the city to form the park as we see it today.

Birding is good year-round, dropping off only in the summer months. Within its boundaries the park provides a mix of woodland, meadow, freshwater marsh and ponds, scrub, flat grassy areas, sandy foreshore and saltwater bay. The best time to visit is early morning.

DIRECTIONS

The park is located on the north side of West 4th Avenue, between Wallace and Discovery Streets. It is served by the #4 and #42 Spanish Banks buses, and is only a short walk from the #7 Dunbar stop at West 4th Avenue and Alma Street. The park can be entered anywhere along its perimeter and cycling is permitted. No cars are allowed, but there is ample parking all around. From Jericho, depending on tides, one can walk west along Spanish Banks to the Point Grey headland or east along rocky Bayswater beach to Kitsilano.

BIRD SPECIES

Winter

October through May are excellent for waterfowl. Between the freshwater ponds and the bay, almost every species of duck may be found, including *Wood Duck*, a few *Eurasian Wigeon* in among the flocks of *American Wigeon, Green-winged Teal, scaup, goldeneye, scoters, mergansers* and *Oldsquaw. Common, Pacific and Red-throated Loons, Horned, Western and Red-necked Grebes* (rarely *Eared Grebe*), and *Pelagic and Double-crested Cormorants* may easily be seen on the bay. Scan the water carefully for such extreme rarities as *Yellow-billed Loon, King Eider and Clark's Grebe. Alcids* are not commonly found, although *Marbled Murrelet* do occur sporadically in winter.

In winter the park's growing rabbit population has attracted **Red-tailed and Cooper's Hawks**, and **Great-horned and Short-eared Owls**. The **Barred Owl** has also been seen here. **Sharp-shinned Hawk** and **Merlin** hunt here, and in some winters **Peregrine Falcon** and **Goshawk** have been seen. **Varied Thrush** and **Northern Flicker** winter in the park and brambley areas shelter **Song and Fox Sparrows**, finches and other shrub loving birds. Flocks of **Pine Siskin** and **American Goldfinch** feeding in the alder occasionally include a few **Common redpolls**.

Summer

In summer, few songbirds remain other than **blackbirds, sparrows** and *finches*. Five species of *swallows (Barn, Cliff, Tree, Violet-green and Northern Rough-winged)* frequent the ponds. On cloudy days **Black and Vaux's Swifts** may be seen. A variety of shorebirds - **sandpipers, yellowlegs** and **dowitchers** - also visit the ponds, especially in return migration starting in July when the water levels fall and the mud is exposed.

Migration

Spring and fall bring many migrating species. In spring mixed feeding flocks of **warblers (Wilson's, Yellow-rumped, Orange-crowned, Yellow** and others**), Warbling Vireo, kinglets** and **chickadees** pass through the woodlots on the eastern side of the park near the ponds, among the trees bordering 4th Avenue and along the Pipeline Trail (which runs along the south side of the west marsh). The **Orange-crowned Warbler** and **Common Yellowthroat** have been known to overwinter in mild winters.

In both spring and fall, **Sora, Virginia Rail** and **Common Snipe** can at times be found in the marsh. **Band-tailed Pigeon**, and **Lincoln's, Savannah and Golden Crowned Sparrows** pass through. The **Northern Shrike** stations itself in the scrub area south of the concrete wharf. Small numbers of **Western Meadowlarks, Horned Larks, Snow Buntings** and **Lapland Longspurs** briefly visit this area later in the fall migration. **Gulls** to be found around the pond or on the bay include **Glaucous-winged, Mew, Ring-billed, California, Thayer's and Bonaparte's**. In late September and early October **Franklin's Gull** is usually seen off the Crab Pier west of the Sailing Club.

Breeding Species

About 20 species breed in the park, including **Willow Flycatcher, Bushtit, White crowned Sparrow, Rufous-sided Towhee, Common Yellowthroat, Mallard, American Coot** and **Pied-billed Grebe**. Some years, the **Red-winged Blackbirds** that nest in the cattails are joined by one or two pairs of **Yellow-headed Blackbirds.**
In total, about 180 species are regularly to be found in the park, and over the years more than 30 accidental species have been recorded.

QUEEN ELIZABETH PARK

Queen Elizabeth Park is located near the centre of the City of Vancouver on one of the highest hills in the city. At the top of the hill is the Bloedel Conservatory, a popular Vancouver tourist attraction which features a wide variety of tropical and desert flora in a dome with a selection of tropical birds. The area was a rock quarry in the early part of the century. When the quarry ceased production it was turned into these magnificent gardens, and the park was named after Queen Elizabeth the Queen Mother.

From the perimeter of the conservatory you can get a panoramic view of the area. To the north, the mountains with Cypress, Grouse and Seymour ski areas tower above the downtown core, the harbour and Stanley Park. To the west is the University of British Columbia, Pacific Spirit Regional Park and the Gulf Islands. Looking south one sees the lowlands of the Fraser Delta, and to the east are Burnaby Mountain and Central Park.

Native trees in the park include Douglas fir, western red cedar, western hemlock and vine maple. There is a large array of introduced trees and shrubs as well as several grassy areas and the gardens.

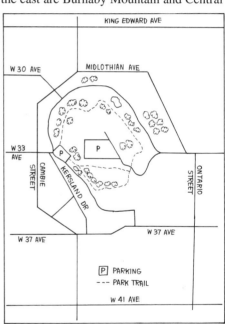

DIRECTIONS

To reach the park from downtown Vancouver, drive south on Cambie Street to 33rd Avenue, turn left, proceed for some 160 m (500 ft) and turn left again into the parking lot. There is a ring road which circles around the north side of the park and goes up to another parking lot which sits atop a major water storage reservoir.

Queen Elizabeth Park

BIRD SPECIES

This park is one of the best spots in Vancouver for migrant passerines. ***Hammond's, Willow*** and ***Pacific Slope Flycatchers, Swainson's and Hermit Thrushes, Solitary and Warbling Vireos, Yellow-rumped, Wilson's, Orange-crowned and Yellow Warblers, Western Tanager*** and ***Lincoln's Sparrow*** are regularly found, as are ***Townsend's and Black-throated Gray Warblers.*** Throughout the park watch the skies for ***five species of swallows***, and on overcast days look for ***Black and Vaux's Swifts.***

Townsend's Solitaire and **Red-naped Sapsucker** are annual in the park. *Calliope Hummingbird* and **Tennessee Warbler** are more rare, but worth looking for in this area. These species are rarely seen elsewhere in the Vancouver area.

Time of day, season and weather play a major part in bird watching in Queen Elizabeth Park. On a pleasant sunny afternoon the park can be virtually devoid of birds. The best time of the year is mid-April through mid-May. The best time of day is usually early morning, although late afternoons can sometimes be productive. The best weather is bad weather - overcast skies, preferably following a storm, can provide an abundance of passerines all around the park.

As you leave the parking lot, follow a pathway southeast along the base of the hillside. Look here for **Swainson's and Hermit Thrushes** in the evergreens and **Golden-crowned and White-crowned Sparrows** along the ground. A radio tower is located up the hillside where the pathway turns left. This area occasionally has **Calliope Hummingbirds** and **Red-naped Sapsucker.** Continue around the south side of the Lawn Bowling Club. The shrubbery here can contain a variety of **warblers (Tennessee Warblers** have been observed here, as have **Black-headed Grosbeaks** and *thrushes*).

The deciduous trees to the east of the Lawn Bowling Club provide shelter for **Bushtits, Black-capped Chickadees,** both **kinglets, Western Tanager, Lincoln's Sparrow** and occasionally **Red Crossblll.**

Proceed northwards crossing the road up to the conservatory and Seasons in the Park restaurant. The deciduous trees below the restaurant can harbour **Yellow, Wilson's, Townsend's, Black-throated Gray and Orange-crowned Warblers**. Watch the tops of the evergreens for **Western Wood-Pewees** and **Olive-sided Flycatchers.**

Continue around to the north and west to the area of the quarry gardens. **Townsend's Solitaire** visit this part of the park every spring. **Band-tailed Pigeon** can sometimes be seen in the treetops. Watch and listen for **Hammond's, Willow and Pacific Slope Flycatchers** in spring migration.

Follow the pathway through the woods around the north and west sides of the qardens. This area can contain **Solitary and Warbling Vireos** as well as an array of **Yellow-rumped** and other **warblers** and *flycatchers.* Proceeding in a southeasterly direction will complete the circle returning you to the parking lot.

You may also wish to walk up the hill to the area around the conservatory for a better view of the gardens and the city, or visit the conservatory itself.

In the southwest part of Vancouver along the Fraser River from Marpole to the Musqueam Indian Reserve you will find the most rural area within the city. It is known as Blenheim Flats or, more simply, the flats. Because of the diversity of habitats the area is home to an exceptional array of bird species.

There are two parks located here - Musqueam on the west and Fraser Foreshore on the east, three golf courses, and considerable private lands much of which are small holdings accommodating stables and horse paddocks. Up until the early 1980s the lands at the foot of Angus Drive were bush complete with frog and salamander ponds and even snowshoe hares! Industrial, park and residential developments have since then changed this area considerably.

The North Arm of the Fraser River is a major boat transportation corridor for log booms, barges and tug boats. The dike was built to channel the river and protect lowlands from flooding.

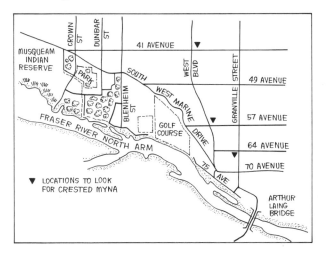

Marpole, Blenheim Flats and Musqueam Park

DIRECTIONS

Car access is available via Angus, Blenheim, Dunbar and Crown Streets and associated side roads (see map). However, one particularly nice feature is that the area is easily accessible by bus . While the private lands of the Marine Drive Golf Course block the opportunity for 7 km (4 mi), good birding is available at both ends. Easy access is possible from 41st Avenue and Crown Street on the west (via the #41 bus) and from the south end of Granville Street on the east (via the #20 bus). Depending on your pace and diversions, these areas can be birded in a couple of hours or you can take a full day! Of the two bus access points, the west end offers the best variety of habitats for productive birding.

The area accessible from 41st Avenue and Crown Street includes habitats of western red cedar and a red alder forest at Musqueam Park, thickets of mixed woods, (including tall cottonwoods and Lombardy poplars) along the horse trail and dike areas, a cattail marsh on the Indian reserve, sloughs, horse pastures and a tidal portion of the Fraser River.

BIRD SPECIES

Birdwatching opportunities change with the season and habitat but a good variety of species can always be found. The annual eulachon run (an anandromous smelt that spawns upstream) occurs during April. The calls of *Bonaparte's Gull* and occasionally *Common Tern* are a sure sign that eulachon are in the river. Other gulls, particularly *Glaucous-winged,* are attracted in numbers. Look for *Mew, Ring-billed, Herring, Thayer's* and other gull species among the loafing flocks settled on the log booms.

Double-crested Cormorant, Common Loon, Western Grebe and other fish eating species including *Common and Red-breasted Mergansers* are often seen on the river. Through the winter months smaller numbers of these species are represented.

Many of Vancouver's common waterfowl species will be found frequenting the sloughs and side channels. *Mallard, Green-winged Teal, Greater Scaup* and *Great Blue Heron* abound. Vegetated shoreline and drainage channels often shelter the *Green-backed Heron. Killdeer* occur in the more open areas and *Spotted Sandpiper* frequent the dike area but are uncommon in winter.

Around the stables and in the horse paddocks *Brewer's and Red-winged Blackbird* and *Brown-headed Cowbird* are always present. Mixed flocks of these species gather especially in winter. The horse paddocks occasionally sport a *Short-eared Owl* or two and *Barn Owl* are reported to reside in some of the stables. *Ring-necked Pheasant* maintain a small population in this area. On the flats you can see raptors including *Red-tailed Hawk, Bald Eagle* and *Cooper's and Sharp-shinned Hawk.*

Musqueam Park has long been known for its forest birds. ***Black-capped and Chestnut-backed Chickadees, Golden-crowned and Ruby-crowned Kinglets, Red Crossbill, Hutton's Vireo, Hammond's Flycatcher*** and ***Western Wood-Pewee*** are regulars in season. Downstream in the alder forest along the horse trail ***Willow Flycatcher, Yellow*** and other ***warblers,*** and ***vireos*** are summer residents. In winter, flocks of ***Pine Siskin*** (occasionally with ***American Goldfinch*** and ***Common Redpoll*** mixed in), ***Fox and Song Sparrows, Varied Thrush, Dark-eyed Junco*** and ***Rufous-sided Towhee*** frequent this habitat. The ***Evening Grosbeak*** is a regular visitor to this area in spring and autumn. Looking for ***Northern Saw-whet, Western Screech and Great-horned Owls in Musqueam Park*** can be particularly rewarding.

Black-capped Chickadee

The horse trail from Musqueam Park to the dike provides excellent birding during the spring migration period. The mixed forest/thicket habitats are excellent for ***warblers, sparrows*** and other small songbirds.

On the Musqueam Indian Reserve, from the intersection of 51st Avenue and Salish Drive, a rough roadway leads south to the Fraser River. West and downstream of this roadway is an extensive marsh, known habitat of the ***American Bittern*** and other marsh frequenting birds. Permission from the Band should be requested before visiting this area.

In summer from June through July, *Black-headed Grosbeak* and *Northern Oriole* are regular breeding species on the flats but their numbers are very small. Tall birch thickets and lombardy poplars are the places to look for these species respectively.

In past years this area of Vancouver has turned up some "firsts." In 1951 the *Ash-throated Flycatcher* was first reported from the Marpole area of southwest Marine Drive and more recently a *Black-and-white Warbler* became a "first" for the Vancouver Natural History Society's Christmas Bird Count.

CRESTED MYNA - This bird, unique to Vancouver, has maintained a small population in the city for nearly a century. In recent years the population has been dropping substantially and *Mynas* are no longer a common sight. Three areas where the *Crested Myna* is still seen regularly are in the vicinities of 41st Avenue and West Boulevard, 57th Avenue and West Boulevard and between 64th Avenue and 70th Avenue on Granville Street. A stroll down back alleys behind the shops will provide the best opportunities. The *Crested Myna* looks like a chunky *European Starling* with conspicuous white wing patches. When not searching for food on the ground it will often perch conspicuously on telephone poles and wires. Its loud raucous calls are very distinctive.

Crested Myna

MAPLEWOOD FLATS CONSERVATION AREA

For over 20 years public interest groups have been lobbying for this prime North Shore waterside wildlife site to be a wildlife sanctuary. In 1992 the owners of the majority of the area - the federal Vancouver Port Corporation - reached an agreement to lease the area for 49 years to Environment Canada to permit the area to be managed as a Wildlife Conservation Area. In the late 1980s the District of North Vancouver which owns important freshwater and saltwater marshlands adjoining the Vancouver Port Corporation land, zoned all of the area "conservation." The whole area is now protected as wildlife and fish habitat. An Environment Canada Science Laboratory Centre will be constructed on 2.5 ha (6.2 ac) in the northeast portion of the area in 1993-94. This facility will provide public washrooms and parking when it opens.

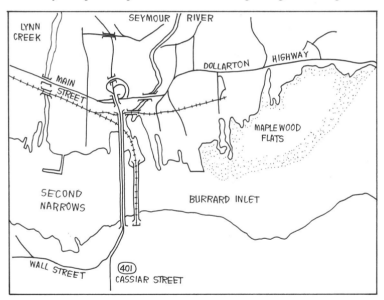

Location of Maplewood Flats, North Vancouver

DIRECTIONS

The Maplewood Flats Conservation Area is approximately 3 km (1.9 mi) east of the north end of the Second Narrows bridge on the south side of Dollarton Highway. Parking is available on the north side of the highway between the Canadian International College and the Crab Shop. This can be reached by public transport from downtown Vancouver by taking a #210 bus going east on Pender to Phibbs Exchange and then transferring to either a #211 or #212 going east on Dollarton Highway. The area can also be reached from downtown Vancouver by taking the Sea Bus to Lonsdale Quay and transferring to a #239 bus to Phibbs Exchange. Transfer to a #211 or #212 bus and ask to be let off at the Crab Shop / Canadian International College.

BIRD SPECIES

This is the last undeveloped waterfront wetland on the north shore of Burrard Inlet. In the past 20 years over 200 species of birds have been observed in the area. There are six habitat types which attract specific species at different times of the year.

Intertidal Flats

On the eastern side of the area are the last intertidal estuarine flats on the North Shore. Large flocks of **American Wigeon, Green-winged Teal** and **Dunlin** with smaller groups of **Gadwall, Northern Pintail, Greater Yellowlegs, Black Turnstone, Mew Gull, Hooded Merganser** and a number of other species winter here. March through May brings **Cinnamon and Blue-winged Teal** and species of **gull, plover** and **sandpipers**. Starting in July many of these species start their fall migration with **sandpipers (Western, Least, Baird's, Pectoral, Spotted and Stilt), plovers (Semipalmated, Black-bellied, Killdeer), dowitcher and yellowleg species, Whimbrel** and **Red - necked phalarope** using the area. In summer bachelor parties of **Common Merganser, Mallard and Harlequin Duck** use the area along with breeding **Belted Kingfisher, Killdeer** and **Spotted Sandpiper**. Vancouver's only breeding pair of **Osprey** have nested here since 1991 and can be watched hunting over the shallow waters sometimes in the company of **Caspian Tern.** Other species of note here are **Eurasian Wigeon, Franklin's Gull** and **Green Heron.**

Deep Saltwater Basin

The deep salt water basin to the south of the rough meadows provides feeding waters for **grebe, loon, cormorant, scaup, scoter, mergansers** and **goldeneye** species in the winter. Species of note are **Harlequin Duck** and **Marbled Murrelet.**

Freshwater Marsh-Pond System

Situated in the northwest corner of the area, on District of North Vancouver land, this system represents an example of remnant natural shoreline. The fresh water flows directly south into brackish marsh and then salt marsh. The thick willow and Pacific crabapple shrub area is a breeding site for **Green-backed Heron, Bewick's Wren,**

Hutton's Vireo and other marsh species. In autumn through spring this pond-marsh is used by ***duck species, Common snipe,*** and the occasional ***American Bittern*** as well as many local songbird species.

(Left to right)   *Blue-winged Teal (male), Cinnamon Teal, Blue-winged Teal (female), Green-winged Teal (male)*

Open Rough Meadow

This area of 20 year old filled-in marsh is ***Savannah Sparrow, American Goldfinch*** and ***White-crowned Sparrow*** breeding habitat in summer. During spring and fall migration the meadow habitat attracts*, **American Kestrel, Western Meadowlarks, Lazuli Buntings** and **American Pipits. Short-eared Owl, Northern Harriers** and **Rough-legged Hawk** also utilize the area on migration. In winter the flocks of **snipe, finches, sparrows, robins** and **flickers** in the area are hunted by **Northern Shrike, Northern Pygmy Owl** and **Merlin**. Other species to be watched for in winter are **Snow Bunting** and **Lapland Longspur**.

Black Cottonwood - Red Alder Forest

The northern part of the area still has remnant floodplain forest which in spring is a feeding area for migrating *warblers, vireos, tanangers* and *thrushes*. In summer look for breeding *Black-headed Grosbeak, Swainson's Thrush, Warbling and Solitary Vireos.* . The winter forest has flocks of *chickadees, nuthatches, kinglets, Hutton's vireos*, and *Varied Thrush* plus *Red-breasted Sapsucker, Hairy Woodpecker* and *Hermit Thrush.*

Broom-Bramble-Alder Bush

Much of the eastern area is covered in thick shrub and young alder which is breeding habitat for *Cedar Waxwing, Western Wood-Pewee, MacGillivray's Warbler* and other songbirds. In winter flocks of *Pine Siskin, House and Purple Finches, Evening Grosbeak* and *Varied Thrush* use the area.

PREDATORY BIRDS

The whole area is used by *Sharp-shinned, Cooper's and Red-tailed Hawks, Bald Eagle, Peregrine Falcon, Merlin, Barred Owl* and *Great-horned Owl.*

For updated information on Maplewood Flats contact Lynn Canyon Ecology Centre at 987-5922.

Cooper's Hawk (male) with dead Steller's Jay

LIGHTHOUSE PARK

Lighthouse Park is situated on Point Atkinson, a rocky headland. The point was named by Captain George Vancouver after Thomas Atkinson, a Royal Navy captain, while engaged in survey work on the southern British Columbia coast in 1792.

In 1873-74 the first lighthouse was built to protect the ships sailing to the logging camps and sawmills on the shores of Burrard Inlet. The stone base of this old wooden tower is still visible to the west of the present lighthouse. In 1881 the 75 ha (195 ac) of crown land to the north of the lighthouse was granted to the Dominion government for a lighthouse reserve.

In 1910 the reserve was leased by the Dominion government to North Vancouver and later leased to West Vancouver upon its incorporation in 1912. Today's Lighthouse Park has remained relatively undisturbed.

The 75 ha (195 ac) of Lighthouse Park contain a remarkable range of natural conditions and varied environments. Approximately two-thirds of the park's perimeter is shore-line consisting of coves, rocky headlands, high granite cliffs and a group of small rocky islands to the northwest of the park. Here we find plants which require little rainfall, such as arbutus, lodgepole pine, and salal.

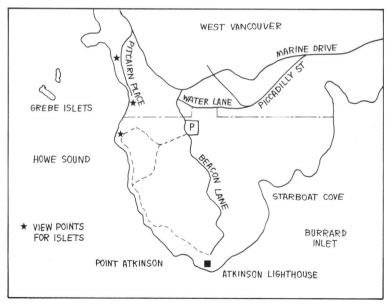

Lighthouse Park and Point Atkinson

The interior of the park is marked by high, rounded granite outcrops (up to almost 120 m above sea level) divided by valleys and narrow draws. The granite outcrops support salal, small Douglas fir, red huckleberry and western sword fern. In the valleys and draws of the park interior where the soil is deeper and seepage water collects stands a magnificent coniferous forest. The largest trees in the valley bottom are Douglas fir, some over 400 years old, 60 m (180 ft) high and 2 m (6 ft) in diameter. Of the younger smaller trees western hemlock and western red cedar are the most abundant with lesser numbers of broadleaf maple and red alder. The shaded forest floor is covered with salal, red huckleberry, hemlock seedlings and western sword fern.

In the smaller valleys where surface water collects and flows to the sea as streamlets during the wetter months the vegetation is particularly luxuriant. These moister areas contain thickets of salmonberry and red alder as well as colonies of Oregon grape, deer fern and various mosses.

DIRECTIONS

To reach Lighthouse Park from Vancouver, drive north over the Lion's Gate Bridge and take the exit to West Vancouver. This exit will lead you to a traffic light at Marine Drive and Taylor Way.   Alternatively you can take the Second Narrows Bridge north from East Vancouver or Burnaby to North Vancouver. Continue west on the Upper Levels Highway (Hwy 1 West) to the Taylor Way exit (Exit 13) then turn left on Taylor Way and proceed south to Marine Drive. From the light at Taylor Way and Marine Drive follow Marine Drive west for 10.3 km (6.4 mi) to Beacon Lane (watch for the Lighthouse Park sign on your left). Turn left on Beacon Lane and follow for 0.3 km (0.2 mi) to the park gate and parking area.

BIRD SPECIES

Over 150 species of birds have visited or reside in the park. The park provides a good variety of sea and land birding opportunities, but because of the rugged terrain visitors must be prepared and alert. Hiking boots or runners will allow you to explore the many steep, rocky trails while common sense will keep you a safe distance from steep cliffs.

In the interior of the park the salmonberry and salal ground cover is a favorite haunt of *Song Sparrow, Rufous-sided Towhee, Dark-eyed Junco* and *Winter Wren*. As you walk the trails listen for **Red-breasted Nuthatch, Bushtit, Varied Thrush** and **Hutton's Vireo** (most vocal from February-April). The open areas (parking area, near the outdoor theatre and along the service road) are good locations to view the forest canopy for **Band-tailed Pigeon, Purple Finch, Evening Grosbeak, Pine Siskin** and **Red Crossbill**. Spring arrivals include **Rufous Hummingbird, Violet-green Swallow,**

Western Tanager and *Swainson's Thrush*. Four species of *flycatchers* summer in the park. The *Hammond's and Pacific-slope Flycatchers* prefer the deep forest, the *Western Wood-Pewee* prefers slightly more open areas while the *Olive-sided Fly-catcher* will often be found high on a conifer snag. *Common Raven, Northwestern Crow* and *Steller's Jay* are the resident corvids while *Brown Creeper, Chestnut-backed Chickadee* and *Golden-crowned Kinglet* all breed in the park and in winter

Golden - crowned Kinglet

form mixed flocks along with *Ruby-crowned Kinglet*. In summer look for *Townsend's Warbler* high in the conifers, *Wilson's and MacGillivray's Warblers* lower in the understorey where they breed and *Yellow-rumped Warbler* which occur only as transients. In early spring one is almost sure to hear the resident *Blue Grouse* booming. Since these birds often call from high in the trees where they are difficult to see it is often advantageous to climb a granite outcrop near a calling bird to gain a better viewpoint. Check the snags in the park as they provide foraging and nesting sites for *Downy, Hairy and Pileated Woodpeckers, Northern Flicker* and *Red-breasted Sapsucker.* The park offers the opportunity to view a few birds of prey including *Bald Eagle, Osprey* (migrant), all *3 species of accipiter* and *Northern Pygmy-Owl* which often calls during the daylight hours. On a nocturnal visit you could also see *Great-horned, Barred, Western Screech and Northern Saw-whet Owl.*

The best location to see shorebirds in or around the park is the Grebe Islets. They are best viewed on a low tide. The two best areas to view the islets are both outside of Lighthouse Park at either the end of Pitcairn Place or Indian Bluff in Kloochman Park. To reach these two areas return to Marine Drive and turn left. The first left (Howe Sound Lane) leads to Kloochman Park; the second left is Pitcairn Place. The trail to Kloochman Park begins just past the Byway on your right (look for sign). *Black Oystercatcher* (resident) are joined in winter by *Surfbird, Black Turnstone* and *Rock Sandpiper* on the islets. *Wandering Tattler* should be looked for during migration in late summer or fall. If you observe the Grebe Islets from Pitcairn Place check the residential plantings for *Anna's Hummingbird* (resident) and *Townsend's Solitaire* (spring migrant).

The cliffs and rock bluffs of the park provide many excellent sites to scan for birds. From Jackpine Point *Common Loons* are abundant in winter with a few summering individuals, *Red-throated and Pacific Loons* are likely in winter while *Yellow-billed Loon* is very rare in winter. From Indian Bluff look for the large rafts of *Western Grebes* and smaller numbers of *Red-necked and Horned Grebes* which congregate near the Grebe Islets in winter. *Double-crested and Pelagic Cormorants* are common residents of the islets while *Brandt's Cormorant* are uncommon in winter. *Harlequin Duck* and *Surf Scoter* can be seen all year while *Greater Scaup, Barrow's and Common Goldeneye, Bufflehead, White-winged Scoter* and *Red-breasted Merganser* are present in winter. Of the gulls which can be seen at the park, the *Glaucous-winged Gull* is a resident. There are *Mew, Thayer's and Herring Gulls* present in the winter while *Bonaparte's Gull* can be seen during spring and fall migration. You should also look for *Common Tern* in the fall. Jackpine Point is a good spot to see alcids. *Marbled Murrelet* and *Pigeon Guillemot* are park residents while *Common Murre* (uncommon) and *Rhinoceros Auklet* (casual) can be seen during the winter.

AMBLESIDE PARK

With the right weather conditions Ambleside Park can be an excellent place to see migrant birds. *Ash-throated Flycatcher, Pygmy Nuthatch, Black-backed Wagtail, Painted Redstart* and *Lark Bunting* have all occurred in this small urban park! *Surf Scoter* is seen in large numbers, and smaller numbers of *Barrow's Goldeneye* and *Harlequin Duck* occur. This park is heavily used by the public and is quite often overrun by dog walkers. To avoid the dogs, an early morning start is essential.

DIRECTIONS

To reach Ambleside Park drive north over the Lions Gate Bridge and take the exit for West Vancouver. The exit on the side of the bridge takes you to Marine Drive (going west). Go west along Marine Drive past the Park Royal Shopping Centre to 15th Street. Turn left (south) over the railroad tracks and then turn left again (east) to Ambleside Park.

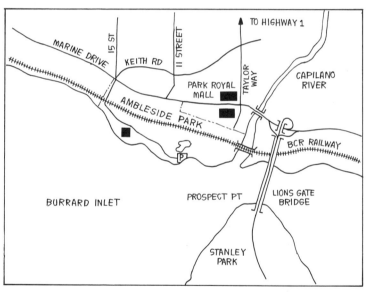

Ambleside Park and First Narrows

BIRD SPECIES

Park in the furthest east parking lot. Directly north of the parking lot are the Ambleside ponds. These should be checked from September to May for *Ring-necked Duck* and and the rare *Tufted Duck* amongst the numerous *Greater and Lesser Scaup.* Other waterfowl usually present include: *Mallard, American Wigeon, Canvasback, Common Goldeneye, Bufflehead,* and the occasional *Hooded Merganser.*

Songbirds are attracted to the bushes and pines at the edge of the ponds. Look for *Harris's and Lark Sparrows*. The ornamental plantings and rough areas to the east and surrounding the ponds can sometimes be alive with migrant passerines, although they are normally quiet.

After checking the ponds walk south to a small rocky spit that juts out into First Narrows of Burrard Inlet. From fall through to spring large numbers of *Surf Scoter* and *Barrow's Goldeneye* congregate. *King Eider* has been seen here on at least a couple of occasions. Also present are smaller numbers of *Common Loon, Red-throated Loon, Red-necked, Horned, and Western Grebes, Double-crested, Pelagic and* sometimes *Brandt's Cormorants, scaup, Harlequin Duck, goldeneyes, Bufflehead, Red-breasted Merganser, Pigeon Guillemot* and *Marbled Murrelet. Oldsquaw,* and *White-winged and Black Scoters* are uncommon. This is one of the few places in the Vancouver area that *Barrow's Goldeneye* and *Harlequin Duck* are found in the summer.

During low tide the gravel bars are exposed. Check the flocks of *Glaucous-winged and Mew Gulls* for *Thayer's and Herring Gulls* in the winter, and *California Gull* in the spring and fall.

Follow the shoreline east from here to reach the Capilano River which is a good spot to see *Common Merganser, Belted Kingfisher* (usually around the railway bridge) and more roosting gull flocks. Sometimes *American Dipper* can be seen some distance upstream from here during winter.

Mount Seymour Provincial Park is a 3,508 ha (8,665 ac) mountain wilderness area in the North Shore mountains. It is bounded on the east by Indian Arm, on the south by North Vancouver, on the west by the Seymour River and the Greater Vancouver Water District watershed and on the north by the Coast Mountain Range. The park includes most of the 1,453 m (4,790 ft) Mount Seymour and nearby Mount Elsay, 1,418 m

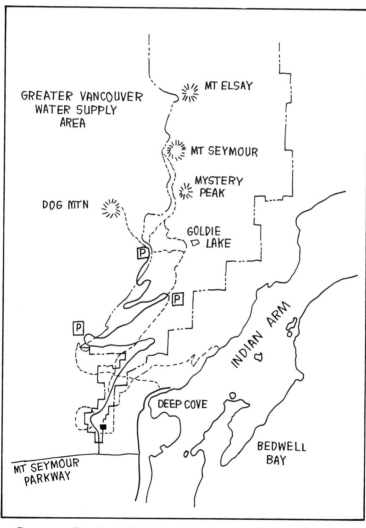

Mount Seymour Provincial Park

(4,680 ft) and Mount Bishop, 1,508 m (4,980 ft). The park encompasses the Coastal Hemlock Zone at elevations below 1,000 m (3,300 ft), and the Mountain Hemlock Zone at elevations above 1,000 m (3,300 ft).

Characteristic vegetation of the Coastal Hemlock Zone includes western hemlock, western redcedar and red alder. Much of the original growth of this zone was logged in the 1920s. The resultant second growth forest is a mixture of deciduous (largely red alder) and coniferous (largely western hemlock).

No logging took place in the Mountain Hemlock Zone so there are significant areas of old growth (mature) mountain hemlock and yellow cedar. The trees and associated shrubs - copper bush and white rhododendron - tend to grow in "islands" separated by shrubs such as red heather and blueberry. The Sitka mountain-ash is important in the sub-alpine areas because it provides berries for birds.

The subalpine zone contains a number of water related habitats including bog vegetation fringing lakes such as Goldie and Flower. Open water is limited mainly to small lakes (Goldie, Elsay). Elsay Lake has been stocked with trout.

Ski runs in the park are covered with sparse pioneer vegetation such as Saxifraga and Luetkea. This habitat is a factor of some importance to bird species such as **Blue Grouse**, which roost in nearby trees, but feed along the ski slope/forest interface in summer and fall.

DIRECTIONS

From east of Vancouver follow Highway 1 (west) over the Second Narrows Bridge. From south of Vancouver, travel north on Boundary Road and watch for the North Shore on-ramp to Highway 1 which again feeds onto the Second Narrows Bridge. Watch carefully for the signs and avoid getting onto the left side lane that takes you off the highway.

Once on the Second Narrows Bridge look for the Mount Seymour Exit signs at the north end of the bridge. You will exit to the right and be on Mount Seymour Parkway. Follow the Parkway along about 7 km (4 mi) to Mount Seymour Road, turn left at the Parkgate Shopping Centre and continue ahead. As soon as you are through the flashing lights, you are in the park. A sign directs you to the Park office where checklists, maps and other information are available (Monday-Friday, normal business hours).

The park highway is 10 km (6.2 mi) long from the entrance at 100 m (330 ft) elevation to the topmost parking area at 1,000 m (3,300 ft).
The network of hiking trails begins at the upper parking lots. Two suggested routes are:

(1) Goldie Lake and associated ponds and bog vegetation; (1-1 1/2 hours return,) and (2) Mystery Peak (including Mystery Lake); (about 2 hours return). The elevation change is 450 m (1485 ft).

Please note that the weather can change very quickly on a mountain top. Be prepared by taking warm clothing and/or rain gear with you. Wear good hiking boots and stay on trails.

BIRD SPECIES

Some 119 species have been recorded as occurring in Mount Seymour Provincial Park. A checklist of the Birds of Mount Seymour Provincial Park is available. An analysis of the list indicates a marked seasonality in species occurrence and altitudinal zonation in bird species.

The species typical of the Western Hemlock Zone in summer are the ***Swainson's Thrush, Warbling Vireo,*** and ***Western Tanager***. The common resident birds include the ***Winter Wren, Varied Thrush,*** and ***Chestnut-backed Chickadee.*** In the Mountain Hemlock Zone common summer residents include the ***Hermit Thrush***, and ***Vaux's Swift.*** Residents include the ***Gray Jay*** and ***Three-toed Woodpecker.***

Rock Ptarmigan (female)

When looked at on the basis of altitudinal zonation, birds may be seen to have lower elevation/sub-alpine counterparts. For example, the ***Black-throated Gray Warbler*** of lower slopes is replaced by the ***Townsend's Warbler*** at higher elevations. Also, the

Swainson's Thrush of lower slopes is replaced entirely by the *Hermit Thrush* in sub-alpine areas.

Most of the specialty birds are sub-alpine species. The *Blue Grouse* is seen at all elevations, commonly along the roadsides. A good time to see them is spring (May, June) when they are hooting. Hens with broods are often seen in summer. *Blue Grouse* make an upward migration to higher altitudes in winter where they live in trees, often high up. Tracks in snow are a good clue to their presence.

The *Rock and White-tailed Ptarmigan* are a recent regular addition to the park the last few years. Mount Seymour is now "the" place to find these birds in winter, especially the valleys between Mystery Peak and 2nd Pump Peak.

The *Northern Pygmy-Owl* is a park resident, but the best time to look for this species is in winter. Numbers vary from year to year. Look along roadsides and trailsides where they often sit in the open. They feed on small birds such as *kinglets* and *chickadees.* Both *Black and Vaux's Swifts* are summer residents here. Good places to see them are the lookout (on the main highway, elevation 850 m (2,800 ft)) and Mystery Peak. They are often seen in numbers when there is a low cloud ceiling. The *Three-toed Woodpecker* is probably a resident sub-alpine species. Goldie Lake and Mystery Lake trails offer good possibilities. The *Gray Jay* is another sub-alpine species. If you have your lunch they will probably find you!

The *Mountain Chickadee* is another sub-alpine species. Look for it at Goldie Lake or Mystery peak. The *Chestnut-backed Chickadee* is generally distributed throughout the park.

The *Black-headed Grosbeak* is a summer resident at lower elevations in mixed woods. The *Rosy Finch* is definitely a "Seymour Specialty" to look for in winter (November - March) in the sub-alpine. Flocks can be seen along roadsides feeding on plant seeds. *Pine Grosbeak* is another winter sub-alpine resident. A number of good sightings have occurred in recent years at Mystery Peak.

Both *Red and White-winged Crossbills* occur throughout the park, the former being more regular in its occurrence and numbers. Mystery Peak is a good place to find both species.

Some 119 species have been recorded for the park, of which 14 are accidentals. Birders should be on the lookout for migrating raptors such as *accipiters, Red-tailed Hawk, Rough-legged Hawk* and *falcons.*

Cypress Provincial Park, along with Mt. Seymour in North Vancouver, provides the most accessible subalpine birding in the Vancouver area. The park, established in 1975 and now almost 3,000 ha (7,410 ac) in size, forms part of the North Shore mountains, the scenic backdrop to Vancouver. An excellent paved road climbs through western hemlock and Douglas-fir forests, eventually reaching more level terrain near the headwaters of Cypress Creek at an elevation of 1,000 m (3,300 ft). At this point you are in the lower reaches of the coastal subalpine forest, known to biologists as the Mountain Hemlock Zone. This zone is famous for its huge accumulations of snow in winter and subsequent late snow melt in spring (and often early summer!). Characteristic trees are mountain hemlock, yellow cedar, amabilis fir, and western white pine. The understory is dominated by ericaceous plants such as red heather, blueberry, huckleberry, false azalea, white rhododendron and copperbush. A number of small lakes and fens add to the natural diversity, and much of the remaining forest is beautiful old growth, with many large trees and snags.

Views are excellent from several places in the park, especially for the more adventurous birders who climb one of the three peaks. Large clearcut areas detract from the scenic beauty, but provide summer habitat for ***Blue Grouse.***

Blue Grouse (male, coastal form)

*Cypress Provincial
Park and
Howe Sound*

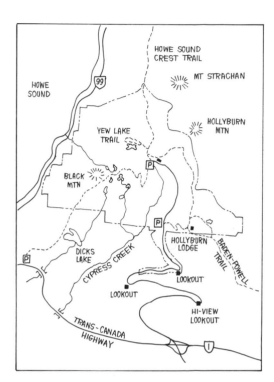

DIRECTIONS

Take the Upper Levels Highway (Highway 1) west from Taylor Way in West Vancouver to the Cypress Provincial Park exit. The road starts at 300 m (990 ft) elevation, climbs gently at first to a tight corner, then more steeply to a second switchback at Hi-View Lookout at an elevation of 525 m (1,730 ft), about 5.3 km (3.3 mi) from the highway. After stopping here, continue up the hill around two more switchback corners, passing the cross-country ski area until the end of the road is reached at the Cypress Bowl ski area. The ski operations are owned and operated by Cypress Bowl Recreations, Ltd., who also provide cafeteria service most of the year. Washrooms are located in the cafeteria building at the parking lot. You have several options once reaching the parking area; indeed there is a myriad of trails in this park.

The Yew Lake trail is an easy 1.5 km (0.9 mi) loop.   Starting at the bases of both chairlifts, this trail follows Cypress Creek through open forest to Yew Lake. At a small fen system near the lake, a boardwalk trail leads you north into a patch of forest and then out onto a logging road in a burn area. A short walk to the northwest provides a good view of Howe Sound and excellent birding, especially during fall migration.

The Howe Sound Crest trail starts at the same point as the Yew Lake trail, but branches off to the right (north) just past the Strachan Mountain chairlift, climbing the ridge quickly and eventually leading (after a long and strenuous hike) to the Lions, perhaps

Vancouver's most scenic mountains. The hike to the Lions should only be attempted by experienced hikers with a good map; the trail is not maintained throughout the length of the ridge.

A section of the Baden-Powell trail leads from the parking lot up the slopes of Black Mountain (1,217 m, 4020 ft), where another loop trail winds around some small subalpine lakes. Another popular hike is up Hollyburn Mountain (1,325 m, 4,370 ft), which can be reached from the cross-country ski area.

BIRD SPECIES

Cypress is best visited from May through October. Make the Hi-View lookout your first stop. It not only offers a magnificent vista of Vancouver (and, on a clear day, Vancouver Island, the Gulf Islands, and North Cascades), but is also a great place to do some tree-top birding. The *Band-tailed Pigeon* is almost always present, perched on top of the cedars and hemlocks below you. *Rufous Hummingbird* (April-June) often perch atop the trees as well, and because they are below you they offer fabulous views of their sparkling colours. In May and June, the trees and shrubs are full of song - *Willow Flycatcher* (June), *Swainson's Thrush, Warbling Vireo, MacGillivray's Warbler, Wilson's Warbler, Orange-crowned Warbler, Black-headed Grosbeak*, and *Western Tanager* are all possible. *Bald Eagles* often sail by.

As you continue up the road, watch for *Blue Grouse* on the roadsides, especially early in the morning. The deep, hooting calls of the males can be heard anywhere along the road in spring, but become more numerous at higher elevations. Stop at the "Giant among trees" (a huge yellow cedar) point of interest near the cross-country ski area junction; this stretch of the road is prime *Red-breasted Sapsucker* habitat. They love the thin-barked hemlocks for drilling sap-wells. In May and early June, listen for their drum-rolls, which, like all sapsucker tattoos, start out fast and end very slowly. Later in the summer, their nests can sometimes be found by listening for the incessant begging calls of the young sapsuckers.

Park at the main downhill ski area parking lot. Listen for the musical whistles of *Fox Sparrow* singing on the slopes just above the parking lot (along the start of the Baden-Powell trail)—this is one of the only places in the Vancouver area where this species breeds. On a slow circuit of the Yew Lake nature trail on a May or June morning you might find *Blue Grouse* (at least heard!), *Vaux's Swift, Red-breasted Sapsucker, Olive-sided Flycatcher, Gray Jay, Steller's Jay, Common Raven, Chestnut-backed Chickadee, Hermit Thrush, Varied Thrush, Orange-crowned, MacGillivray's, and Wilson's Warbler, Red Crossbill* and more. Try whistling like a *Northern Pygmy-Owl* here (or anywhere in the Cypress Bowl area); you will at least attract mobbing passerines if not the diminutive owl itself.

A side trip to the burn area northeast of Yew Lake is often worth taking, especially in August and September, when raptor migration brings **Sharp-shinned, Cooper's, and Red-tailed Hawks, Northern Harrier, American Kestrel**, and perhaps other species using the updrafts on the mountain slopes and cutting through the Cypress Creek valley shortcut to the rest of the North Shore mountain ridges. A longer hike up the Howe Sound Crest trail could yield more subalpine specialties, notably **Three-toed Woodpecker** - this is the most consistent site for this species in the Lower Mainland.

Winter and early spring have their charms here, but you will usually have to stick to the roads if you do not want to don your skis or snowshoes to enter the forests. As well, the winter forests are rather silent except for a few chattering flocks of **Chestnut-backed Chickadees** and **Golden-crowned Kinglet** or the croak of a **Common Raven** overhead. Winter is the best time of year to see the **Gray Jay; Northern Pygmy-Owl** and **Red-breasted Sapsucker** can occasionally be seen.

Steller's Jay

REIFEL BIRD SANCTUARY · 45

Reifel Bird Sanctuary is situated at the mouth of the South arm of the Fraser River less than an hours drive from the city of Vancouver. It is 8 km (5 mi) west of Ladner on Westham Island in Delta. The Sanctuary is run by the non-profit B.C. Waterfowl Society. The Society maintains the sanctuary and encourages appreciation of wetland wildlife habitat in the Fraser River estuary.

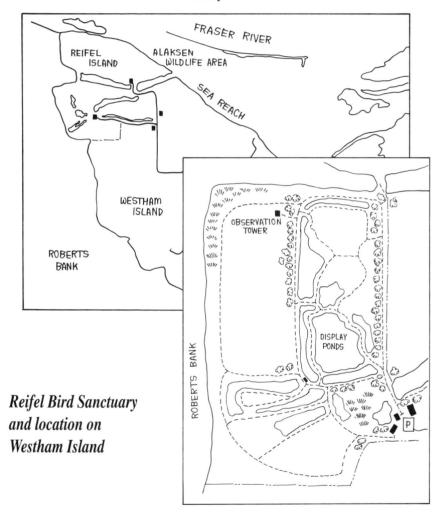

Reifel Bird Sanctuary
and location on
Westham Island

The Reifel Bird Sanctuary is named after George C. Reifel who purchased the north end of Westham Island in 1927. By 1929 most of the diking and reclamation work was completed and he built the family home. Initially grain was grown on the farm, but in World War II his son, George H. Reifel, grew much needed sugar beet seed. On 202 ha (500 ac) the farm supplied one-third of the country's demand in 1961.

Largely as a result of the efforts of conservationists Barry Leach and Fred Auger, the B.C. Waterfowl Society was formed. The Society leased some land from the Reifels to manage it as a bird sanctuary. Ducks Unlimited created numerous ponds and islands on some of the diked land to enhance the area for waterfowl nesting and loafing. The provincial Government purchased additional foreshore bringing the total sanctuary area to 344 ha (850 ac).

The Federal Government bought the Reifel farm in 1973. The British Columbia Waterfowl Society now leases this crown land from the Canadian Wildlife Service.

The sanctuary is on the Fraser River floodplain If the area was not diked it would flood on every high tide as would the rest of Westham Island. The sanctuary itself has about 3 km (1.9 mi) of trails most of which are on dikes. The dikes give a little height to view across otherwise flat areas. All the waterways and ponds are controlled to maximize bird use; some areas are dry in summer then flooded slowly for shorebirds in spring and fall then, completely flooded for ducks and geese in winter. Water comes in at high tide under control and flows out at low tide. This means much of the sanctuary is brackish. The three sloughs on the east side of the sanctuary are freshwater.

Westham Island is prime agricultural land. Farmers grow a wide variety of crops including potatoes, corn, grain, cabbage, strawberries and raspberries. The 1 km (0.6 mi) driveway into the sanctuary parking lot is lined by alder and blackberry with a few coniferous and Pacific crabapple. The eastern sloughs (Robertson, Fuller, Ewan) are bordered by willows and Pacific crabapple. The central area has lots of shrub cover and Douglasfir and black cottonwood. The outer west dike is more sparse and open. An extensive cattail marsh stretches out to the west and the Strait of Georgia. The highest tides in this area reach 4.8 m (16 ft) while the lows go down to 1.2 m (2 ft).

DIRECTIONS

From Highway 99 follow signs to Ladner then continue west out of Ladner on 47A. After a short time the road changes its name to River Road West. Follow River Road for 2.9 km (1.8 mi) turning right onto Westham Island bridge. Follow Westham Island Road for 4.8 km (3 mi) until you arrive at two sets of gates. Take the left hand turn and follow the driveway for 1 km (0.62 mi) to the parking lot.

The Reifel Bird Sanctuary has wheelchair accessible washrooms, picnic tables and a gift shop selling a variety of items from chocolate bars to bird seed. There is a collection of 250 stuffed birds which can be viewed on weekends or by arrangement. Guided tours are offered to pre-booked groups of 8 or more people giving them a group rate of adults $1.00, children and seniors $0.50. Every Sunday at 10:00 a.m. a guided tour is offered to the public. The Sanctuary is open every day from 9:00 a.m. - 4:00 p.m. with admission for adults of $3.25, and children (2-14 yrs) and seniors (60+) $1.00.

BIRD SPECIES

The mixed habitats at the sanctuary have supported 253 species of birds. In winter, waterfowl and raptors are at their best. A flock of 25,000 **Snow Geese** come in by mid October from Wrangel Island, Siberia; they can be found offshore at low tide and often in the fields at high tide. Many wintering ducks and shorebirds follow the same pattern of being out in the intertidal areas at low tide and flying in at high tide.

Over 24 **duck** species have been recorded and three **merganser** species can often be found in winter. **Eurasian Wigeon** can be seen most days in winter on the sloughs and fields feeding with the **American Wigeon**.

A few pair of **Wood Duck** and **Ring-necked Duck** may also be seen. Large flocks of **Trumpeter Swan** (high count of 600), plus a few **Tundra Swan** feed offshore and on Westham Island in winter.

Summer attracts **Cinnamon Teal** and **Blue-winged Teal** along with large numbers of **Gadwall** which after **Mallard** are the most common breeding duck. **Northern Pintail, American Wigeon,** and **Northern Shoveler** also attempt to breed but in very small numbers. Large flocks of **Canada Geese** moult in the area in July and August and up to 2000 can be seen on Westham Island.

Peak migration times at the Sanctuary are April, May and August through October. In April there is a high influx of fish eating birds at the river mouth and offshore feeding on eulachon. Up to 2,000 **Pacific Loon** and other **loon** species gather offshore to feed before moving north to breeding areas. **Red-breasted and Common Mergansers** also gather here along with hundreds of **Bald Eagles** and **Double-crested Cormorants**. Many **gulls** also come in but are quite hard to identify due to the distance out from the sanctuary.

Shorebirds are also eager to get north during this period. Many shorebirds such as **Dunlin, Western Sandpiper, Black-bellied Plover** and **dowitcher**, pass through in April. . Some can be seen in the west field at high tide resting or feeding offering a closer look at their fresh plumage.

Thirty-six species of shorebirds have been seen at the sanctuary from the rare **Spotted Redshank** and **Temminck's Stint** to the more regular but uncommon **Ruff, Sharp-tailed, Baird's, and Solitary Sandpipers.** The first **Western Sandpipers** of the fall start south in late June followed by **Least** and a few **Semipalmated Sandpipers**. Later in July and August larger numbers of **Greater and Lesser Yellowlegs** along with **Long- and Short-billed Dowitchers** also start to move south.

Sharp - tailed Sandpiper

The passerines follow a similar pattern of appearance at the sanctuary.. Although *warblers, flycatchers* and other passerines start a little later in mid-May, they do not return until August. One of the better areas for passerines is the northeast corner and slough walk just east of the parking lot. The *winter sparrows -   White-crowned, Golden-crowned, Fox and Song* can be found along the east dike. Lucky observers may find *Lincoln's, Swamp, White-throated and Harris' Sparrows* on any trail.

The *Black-crowned Night Heron*, a bird which is very hard to find in the Vancouver area, has turned up at least seven consecutive winters on Fuller Slough. They often sit on the sunny side of the slough in willows. *Green-backed Herons* are also seen through the sanctuary from August to the end of September.

Many birds of prey can be seen at Reifel. *Red-tailed Hawk, Bald Eagle, Coopers Hawk, Northern Harrier, Great-horned and Barn Owl* all breed in this area. *Rough-legged Hawk, Gyrfalcon* and *Snowy Owl* come down from the north to winter in this area. *Peregrine Falcon, Merlin, Sharp-shinned Hawk* and *Northern Saw-whet Owl* are seen regularly throughout the winter. The *Turkey Vulture* and *American Kestrel* are seen on passage and rarely stay more than a few days. The first *Black-shouldered Kite* in Canada was seen here in April 1990.

Ladner Harbour Park

As you travel down River Road towards Ladner it may be worth a brief stop at Ladner Harbour Park. The turning into the park is approximately 400 m (3,320 ft) after Ferry Road. There is a mixture of deciduous woodland here with a number of large cottonwoods. A broad spectrum of passerines may be found here including *west coast warblers, vireos, Evening Grosbeak*, and *Western Tanager.* Good views of *Cliff, Barn, Violet-green and Tree Swallows* can also be made. But in particular this is a generally reliable area for *Northern Oriole* (Bullock's race), particularly in the area immediately adjacent to the warden's hut. The *Swamp Sparrow* has recently been recorded in this locality in the winter. The park has also been home to *Blue Jay.*

Black - crowned Night Heron

Westham Island

On leaving Ladner on River Road West, the series of sharp bends near 3653 River Road is worth pausing at to see *Mourning Dove*. In particular peer through the chain-link fencing over the area where boat houses are being constructed. After turning right onto Westham Island Road and crossing the single lane wooden bridge (extremely slippery when wet) pull up on the immediate right. Walk back onto the bridge and view Canoe Pass. In the fall and winter, *Red-necked, Western, and Horned Grebes, Common and Barrow's Goldeneye,* and various other diving ducks can be seen, and on rare occasions in late spring, one or two *Mute Swan.*

All of the lands of Westham Island are private property, including the dikes, please do not trespass on this area. The first turning on the left is Trim Road which gives good views over Canoe Pass. At low tide a mud bank appears which particularly in the winter holds good numbers of *gull* species. The dead tree along Trim Road is a good raptor perch and along with the more regular *Bald Eagle* and *Red-tailed Hawk*, rarer species including *Peregrine Falcon, Merlin* and *Kestrel* can be observed, and on extreme rare occasions both *Gyrfalcon* and *Prairie Falcon* have been observed in the winter. Also in the winter scan the fields from Trim Road, particularly towards the extreme northwest as *Snowy Owl* has been observed here.

Tamboline Road is approximately 1.4 km (0.9 mi) further along Westham Island Road on the left. . The dikes may hold *Snipe* in fall-winter-spring, and various dabbling ducks in spring and summer including all three species of *teal.* During warbler migration, suitable weather conditions can yield a varied "fall-out" in the many hedges and trees. The reeded dike 0.8 km (0.5 mi) along on the left-hand side at #4380 is a good location to look for over-wintering *Lincoln's Sparrow*. Large numbers of *Golden-crowned Sparrow* can be found along this stretch, with *White-crowned and Fox Sparrows* during spring migration. The junction of Tamboline Road and Westham Island road is a good location to watch for *Barn Owls* at dusk. Several pairs breed in barns on the island.

In fall and winter the fields of Westham Island can be teeming with wildfowl but due to the pressures of hunting the birds tend not to be present during the daytime. However, outside the hunting season the views can be spectacular. Peak numbers of *Snow Geese* can reach 30,000 plus. *Trumpeter and Tundra Swans* can number up to 500 in the area. Many can be observed feeding in farm fields at high tide. The predominant duck species is *American Wigeon* and high numbers of *Eurasian Wigeon* can also be seen. A high count of 100 male *Eurasian Wigeon* was made in a flock of approximately 3,000 *American Wigeon* in February 1989. The slough near the children's playfield is worth pausing at, as both *Hooded and Common Mergansers* may be seen here at close quarters.

ROBERTS BANK JETTY,
TSAWWASSEN FERRY TERMINAL
AND BRUNSWICK POINT

The Roberts Bank Superport jetty was built in the late sixties. It is a 5 km (3.1 mi) long jetty with a bulk coal loading facility at the end. This is the largest bulk loading terminal on the west coast of North America. The facility is operated by Westshore Terminals Limited. The coal is shipped to Pacific Rim countries such as Japan, Korea, and Taiwan. The coal is brought by Canadian Pacific and Canadian National Railways unit trains from southeastern British Columbia and from Alberta. Sometimes the presence of all this rolling stock can make birding difficult, but generally most of the jetty is accessible by car. However, if the birding is slow, you can always do a bit of train spotting. Birders are reminded that the trains are operated electronically while they are on the jetty, so beware. They can move at any time!

The Tsawwassen Ferry Terminal was built in the mid-sixties. From here ferries sail to Vancouver Island and the Gulf Islands. The ferries to Vancouver Island go to either Swartz Bay, which is north of Victoria, or to Nanaimo.

The point of land immediately south of Canoe Pass, and south of Westham Island, is known to Vancouver birders by the unofficial name of Brunswick Point.

The western side of this area is formed by the Strait of Georgia. Roberts Bank itself forms part of the deltaic deposits of the Fraser River while Brunswick Point contains an extensive cattail marsh. The farmlands above the high tide level are protected by an extensive system of dykes. These farmlands are flat and featureless and the fields are surrounded by drainage ditches and in some places by hedgerows. Corn is the main crop that is grown, but there are fields given over to potatoes and cereals.

DIRECTIONS

Highway 99 runs from downtown Vancouver to the U.S.A./Canadian border. Just south of the Massey Tunnel, Highway 17 branches off to the south. To reach the Roberts Bank jetty, proceed south on Highway 17 from this intersection. After 2.1 km (1.3 mi) you will reach a set of traffic lights that are at the intersection with Highway #10. Continue south for another 2.9 km (1.8 mi) on Highway 17. You will see a sign that directs you to the Roberts Bank Superport. Exit here and go 1.9 km (1.2 mi) on Delta Port Way, turn left on 53rd Street and go 0.6 km (0.4 mi) before turning right on 28th Avenue. Then follow the main road 3.6 km (2.2 mi) to the base of the Roberts Bank jetty.

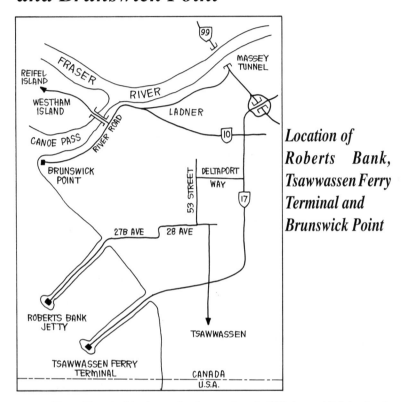

Location of Roberts Bank, Tsawwassen Ferry Terminal and Brunswick Point

The Tsawwassen Ferry Terminal is situated at the south end of Highway 17. It is clearly posted on the road signs along this highway.

Brunswick Point can be reached by driving to the far west end of River Road in Delta, past the turnoff to Westham Island, and then walking along the dike.

There is a small parking lot on the left hand side at the base of the Roberts Bank jetty. One way to explore the area is to park here and then walk up one side of the jetty and down the other. This will ensure that you see most of the birds that are present. However, if time, energy, or both are limited, you can explore the whole jetty from your car. It is also possible to walk from the base of the Roberts Bank jetty, northwards along the dike to Brunswick Point, or southwards along the dike towards the Tsawwassen Indian Reserve which is clearly marked as a no trespassing area.

Over the years, increasing areas of the Roberts Bank jetty have become accessible to birders, a reversal of the situation that has occurred in many of the other birding areas. Thus, birders are asked to respect the remaining 'No Trespassing' signs so we can continue to come to this area.

BIRD SPECIES

Intertidal Areas

In the area between the Roberts Bank jetty and the Tsawwassen Ferry Terminal, the water is tidal and the level of the tide will have a considerable influence on the distribution of the birds. When the tide is low, the shorebirds and *herons* all feed on the mudflats, which extend most of the way out along the jetty. However, when the tide comes up the mudflats disappear and the shorebirds are replaced by *ducks* and *loons.*

Near the far end of the south side of the jetty there is a small area where you can park. From here you can survey a bay that the tugboats use when they are not helping the large colliers in and out of the docking facilities. *Gulls* and *terns* are common in this sheltered area.

Winter is the season when the most birds are normally present. *Common Loon* live up to their name and very rarely a *Yellow-billed Loon* can be found. *Horned Grebe* are common and there will be the occasional *Eared Grebe*. Waterfowl are abundant with large flocks of *Northern Pintail*, and *American Wigeon* with as many as 20 drake *Eurasian Wigeon* scattered amongst them. We will leave the count of the female *Eurasian Wigeon* for keen birders to determine for themselves. All three species of *scoters* are found, with *Surf Scoter* being the most numerous. Good numbers of *Greater Scaup* are also often present. *Bald Eagle* commonly sit on the tall hydro poles and make excellent subjects for keen photographers. Several hundred *Black-bellied Plover* frequent the mudflats in winter along with large flocks of *Dunlin*. If you search carefully through these winter flocks, you may be able to find the occasional *Western Sandpiper.*

In spring, large flocks of *Brant* may cover the water as they feed on the eel grass that is found the area. Many shorebirds such as *Western, Least, and Baird's Sandpipers* can be found during both spring and fall migrations. The shorebirds are often harassed by *Peregrine Falcon* and *Merlin.*

In early summer the waters are generally fairly empty but large flocks of *Great Blue Heron* feed on the tidal flats. On May 23, 1992, 400 of these birds were seen feeding here. This is the greatest number of the *Great Blue Heron* reported feeding at a single location in the Vancouver area. These herons come from the large heronry at Point Roberts, Washington, a site that may soon be threatened by the development of recreation facilities in the immediate area.

Birders are always on the lookout for rarities, and the Roberts Bank jetty is a good place to find them. A ***Burrowing Owl*** was seen on the jetty. A juvenile ***Sabine's Gull*** was seen sitting on the south side of the jetty on the gravel road that runs beside the railway tracks.

The waters on the north side of the jetty have essentially the same birds as can be seen from the south side. However, at the far end of the north side of the jetty is a mudbank that provides an excellent roosting area for ***gulls*** and ***terns***. To reach this area go 2.2 km from the railway crossing at the base of the jetty, turn right on to a gravel road, then turn left and drive for 1.8 km (1.1 mi) before bearing to the right, following along beside the railway tracks. Stop anywhere in this general area and walk down to the foreshore. ***California and Ring-billed Gulls*** are common in the late summer, as are ***Caspian and Common Terns. Elegant Tern*** were also found roosting here in the late summer and early fall of 1992. ***Long-billed Curlew*** has been seen here, as well as ***Great Egret*** and other rarities.

Take care when walking on the north side of the mudflats. Years ago there were signs along the foreshore warning of quicksand in the area. Over the years the signs have disappeared, but it is unlikely that the quicksand has done likewise!

Farmlands

The farmlands are at the base of the Roberts Bank jetty. During the winter of 1991-92 the hydro-substation and large power poles were favourite perches of a ***Gyrfalcon***. A ***Prairie Falcon*** has also frequented this area in recent years. In season it is possible to observe five different species of ***falcons*** on a single day in this general area. A ***Cattle Egret*** also spent the 1991-92 winter feeding among the cattle on 41B Street near the intersection with 28B Avenue. The hedgerows along the dike in this area can yield many ***sparrows*** and other small passerines. At high tide the fields contain roosting shorebirds and the accompanying raptors.

The traffic can be very heavy on the Tsawwassen Ferry Terminal jetty so it is very dangerous to view birds from the car. It is possible to park in the lot by the terminal for one hour without having to pay, and then bird on foot. ***Jaegers*** and ***terns*** are common in late summer and numerous ***cormorants*** roost on the rocky breakwater. One ***Short-tailed Shearwater*** was seen in 1977 from the ferry just after it had left the terminal. However, if mention of such a pelagic bird at this location should excite you, bear in mind that the Strait of Georgia is essentially barren of pelagics. David Mark, in his book *Where to Find Birds in British Columbia*, comments that he has seen only one pelagic species (***Sooty Shearwater***) in close to 100 round trips on the ferry. This author's experience is little better, having made a few less trips and seeing only two *Fork-tailed Storm Petrel* in 1990, midway between Nanaimo and Horseshoe Bay.

There is a gravel road that runs along the south side of the jetty. Sometimes *Snow Bunting* can be seen along this road in season. Also search the rocky shoreline, as *Black Oystercatcher, Black Turnstone, Surfbird*, and even *Rock Sandpiper* have all been seen on the jetty. The *Black Oystercatcher* may be breeding somewhere in the area while the *Rock Sandpiper* comes as a winter visitor.

Brunswick Point is an excellent birding spot from at least September through May, when large numbers of waterfowl are present. The main attractions are *swans* and *Snow Goose.* Up to 400 swans (mainly *Trumpeter*) concentrate here from November to March, and up to 10,000 *Snow Goose* can be seen from October to April, although

Snow Geese at Roberts Bank

the geese are much less predictable. Since the late 1980s, most of the swans feed on Westham Island during the day, but they return to Brunswick Point in impressive flights to roost for the night. Thousands of dabbling ducks, often including several *Eurasian Wigeon,* feed in the marshes and mudflats around the point. The waterfowl can be seen better at high tide, when they are forced closer to the dike. Flocks of up to 10,000 *Dunlin* can be seen feeding on the flats or flying by in dense masses. Canoe Pass itself usually has rather few birds, which include *Western Grebe, Double-crested Cormorant, Bufflehead*, and *Common and Red-breasted Mergansers*.

The farm fields inside the dike are excellent for birds of prey, including many *Red-tailed and Rough-legged Hawks, Northern Harrier*, and *Bald Eagle. Peregrine Falcon* and *Merlin* are often seen, and some winters, a *Gyrfalcon* or *Prairie Falcon* may be present. Scan the fields and the treetops often as you walk along the dike.

Some of the most interesting birds can be found in the shrubs and dense weed patches just outside the dike. This is a regular spot for the *American Tree Sparrow,* and there are several records of *Swamp Sparrow*. A *Short-eared Owl* may burst out of the shrubbery, and *Snowy Owl* is possible along the dike or sitting on a log out in the marsh. The birder who is not loath to slog through the marsh in rubber boots may flush an *American Bittern*, and get closer looks at *sparrows* and *Marsh Wrens.* Do not wander too far from the dike unless you take care not to get cut off by the rising tide.

The Brunswick Point area can produce some interesting birds during spring and fall migration. Especially worth checking are the shrubby thickets and tall poplars just near the west end of River Road, although a large area of brush has recently been destroyed. The remaining brush can produce a variety of *sparrows* and *warblers* in season, including *Lincoln's* and even the rare *White-throated Sparrow*, and occasionally *Long-eared* or other *owls.* This isolated patch of vegetation could function as a "vagrant trap"; Vancouver's first *Tropical Kingbird* appeared nearby in the fall of 1990. *Horned Lark, Lapland Longspur,* and *Snow Bunting* may be seen along the dike in early spring or late fall. Spectacular concentrations of *Western Sandpiper*, with smaller numbers of other shorebirds, can be seen on the point in spring and fall (especially in the last week of April), and small flocks of the locally rare *White-fronted Goose* occasionally stop on the point in late April or early May.

Point Roberts is a premier spot to look for seabirds in the Greater Vancouver area. *Sooty Shearwater, Short-tailed Shearwater, Brown Pelican, King Eider, Red Phalarope, Long-tailed Jaeger, Little Gull, Sabine's Gull, Black-legged Kittiwake* and *Cassin's Auklet* have all been reported here.

DIRECTIONS

From Vancouver, take Highway 99 south and take the Highway 17 exit heading towards Tsawwassen. At the second set of lights (56th Street) turn left (south) and continue along this till you reach the international boundary. The U.S. side is Point Roberts. Please note that overseas visitors require a visa to enter the United States.

From the international boundary continue south along Tyee Road (the road you are now on) for approximately 3.5 km (2.2 mi) to A.P.A. Road. Turn left (east) and continue for 2.5 km ((1.5 mi) until you see a cemetery on your right. Park here off the road along the row of tall Douglas fir bordering the cemetery. In front of you will be a gate and a path that ends in 200 m (660 ft) at the top of a sand cliff. This is Lily Point which has a great view of Boundary Bay. *Scoters, Barrow's Goldeneye*, and a few *loons* and *grebes* can be seen from this high vantage point in winter.

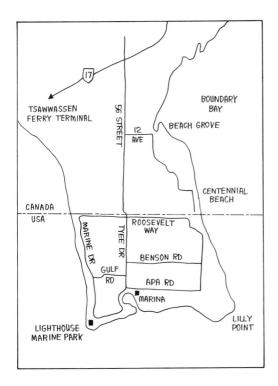

Point Roberts

BIRD SPECIES

To the left of your parked car is a large clearing overgrown with alder, blackberry and other shrubs bordered by second growth deciduous forest. Especially during migration, many songbirds can be seen or heard along the perimeter of the clearing. *Downy Woodpecker, Northern Flicker,   Black-capped and Chestnut-backed Chickadees, Bewick's Wren, Winter Wren, kinglets, vireos, warblers, sparrows* and *finches* are seen in the appropriate season. This is also a very good location for *Hutton's Vireo* all year, but mainly in March and April when territorial singing occurs. These birds respond to a "pishing" sound very well so be sure to try this. Scan the skies for *Red-tailed Hawk, Sharp-shinned and Cooper's Hawks*, especially during migration.

Pileated Woodpecker and *Red-breasted Nuthatch* can be seen with some luck in these mature woods by walking along the paved road that turns south just before the cemetery. This road is very good for songbirds all year round but like most areas can be quiet during winter. Listen for *Red Crossbill* and *Pine Siskin* flying overhead.

Alternatively, good woodland birding can be enjoyed by turning left onto Benson Road and checking the extensive woodlots south and north of this road. Walking the residential sections of this area is also worthwhile. The birds that occur here are similar to those found at A.P.A. Road.

At the end of Tyee Road turn left onto Gulf Road, and then left onto Marina Drive which turns onto Edwards Drive. Approximately 1 km (0.6 mi) along Edwards Drive you will come to a filled gravel pit on your right. Turn onto the gravel road leading to the gravel pit to park. *Scaup, Canvasback, goldeneyes*, and *Bufflehead* frequent the gravel pit from October to April. *Glaucous-winged and Mew Gulls* also occasionally frequent the gravel pit and these should be checked for the odd *California or Thayer's Gulls.*

Surrounding the gravel pits are weedy fields bordered by blackberry hedgerows. By walking along the hedgerows and "pishing' or "squeaking", October to April, you can find *Rufous-sided Towhee, Fox Sparrow, Song Sparrow, Golden-crowned Sparrow and White-crowned Sparrow,* and occasionally a *Lincoln's Sparrow* (frequent during migration). The weedy fields have *American Goldfinch, House Finch, Savannah Sparrow* (rare in winter). In the wetter areas you can find *Common Yellowthroat* and *Common Snipe. Northern Shrike* and raptors occasionally frequent this area. *American Pipit, Lapland Longspur* and *Snow Bunting* occur where weeds have managed to take a foothold in the gravel along the edges of the pond, ditches and road.

Continue west along Edwards Drive for another 1 km (0.6 mi) towards Lighthouse Marine Park, an excellent location to view seabirds. On your right will be a small campground surrounded by pines. During migration these pines can attract songbirds including the occasional *Mountain Chickadee* (fall). Drive into the park on your left and go to the parking area by the beach. Be sure to bring some money for the parking fee. Although many birds frequent the shoreline, this area is mostly productive for a stationary "seabird watch" using a spotting scope.

A path running south along the shoreline takes you to the point itself and the lighthouse which is a good spot to scan from. The summer months are very quiet here with only the occasional *Common Loon, Surf and White-winged Scoter*, or perhaps a summering seaduck. A feeding *Pigeon Guillemot* or *Marbled Murrelet* can also be seen. By the end of August things are quite different. *Common Tern* and *Parasitic Jaeger* arrive at the end of August and are present until the end of October (*Common Terns* arrive and leave earlier than jaegers). The *Parasitic Jaeger* is often seen harassing *Bonaparte's or California Gull*. The *California Gull* begins to show up in August (usually offshore) but by the end of October is absent except for the occasional straggler. The *Bonaparte's Gull* arrives and leaves at approximately the same time, but occasionally straggles into winter. Both the *Arctic Tern* and *Pomarine Jaeger* are very rare here. *Little Gull, Sabine's Gull* and *Black-legged Kittiwake* are occasionally seen.

From late September until early November check the gulls roosting on the pylons for *Heerman's Gull.* The *Common Murre* and *Rhinoceros Auklet* (rare) start to show up at this time as well with the *Common Murre* increasing its numbers throughout the winter. By the first week of May both of these species are difficult to find.

Pelagic Cormorant

Pelagic and Double-crested Cormorants occur all year round while *Brandt's Cormorant* occurs from September to April. *Common, Pacific, and Red-throated Loon*, and *Western, Red-necked, and Horned Grebe* begin to show up in early September but do not occur in larger numbers till the beginning of October. *Eared Grebe* is rare at this location (White Rock pier is a much more reliable location). *Yellow-billed Loon* is also very rare here but worth looking for.

Shorebirds can be seen along the beach during low tide. *Dunlin, Black-bellied Plover, Sanderling* and *Black Turnstone* are the species most often seen. Occasionally, flocks of *Red-necked Phalarope* are seen resting off the point or flying by the tip from mid-August to October.

From mid-October to late February sea ducks are found in large numbers: *Brant, Greater Scaup, Oldsquaw, Black, Surf and White-winged Scoters, Common and Barrow's Goldeneye, Bufflehead, Harlequin Duck* and *Red-breasted Merganser*. Also seen, usually in the early morning, are *Snow Goose* and *Trumpeter Swan*, usually flying overhead.

From late November to late February keep a sharp lookout for *Ancient Murrelet* as this is the most reliable place to see this bird in the Vancouver checklist area. In September also be sure to scan the skies for the *Turkey Vulture* which can sometimes be seen migrating south in small flocks.

From Lighthouse Park, Edwards Drive becomes Marine Drive as it swings north. Go north along Marine Drive for approximately 2 km (1.2 mi) to Front Street on the left. Here at the Breakers Pub parking lot scan for seabirds and check the *cormorants* and *gulls* roosting on the pylons.

Common Goldeneye

BEACH GROVE AND CENTENNIAL PARK

This small area borders the western perimeter of Boundary Bay and because of the historical development of the area, combining agriculture, early cabin country and more recently new rural development, there is an interesting diversity of habitat for new birders to observe many species of birds at relatively close range, as well as giving the experienced birder an opportunity to chase down some rare species.

Beach Grove and Centennial Beach still maintain many of the old conifers and deciduous trees combined with native brush and garden habitat. Walking some of the older side streets, during the spring and fall migrations and the entire winter season will produce most of the west coast *sparrows, warblers, northern finches* and other common land birds.

Beach Grove Park and adjacent woodlots create an active all season corner, with *Barn, Great-horned and Western Screech-Owls* there on a regular basis. The old black cottonwood stand adjacent to the

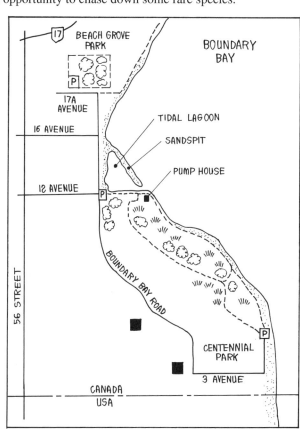

Beach Grove Park and Centennial Park

beach is also a winter resting place and roost for at least 25 *Bald Eagles.* The short drive from the foot of 12th Avenue to Centennial Beach community passes through farmland with some good hedges and brushy treed stands. While the road is narrow with limited parking it will be upgraded in the future allowing safer pull off areas to view the flooded fields and scan the fence posts in winter.

It is the dike walk from the foot of 12th Avenue, with good parking facilities, that is the main attraction to local birders. This 1- 3 km (0.6-1.8 mi) walk begins in a treed and grassy area, opening up in only 50 m (165 ft) to a shallow intertidal lagoon on the left and old grass farmland on the right, interspersed with drainage ditches and small stands of alder and birch trees. Walking the dikes will take the birder to the open bay with its huge expanse of intertidal mudflats and sandbars supporting good eelgrass meadows that are so critical to the wintering **Brant** as well as the spring herring spawn and its associated feeding birds.

Birding the shoreline and the bay is very dependent on tidal conditions. Inside the dike the habitat quickly turns to a combination of old grasses and marshes that eventually opens up at its southern extremity into an interesting Savannah marsh habitat divided into mini-ecosystems by the old sand berms running parallel to the foreshore.

At the southern end of this area Centennial Beach abuts the 49th parallel border with the United States at Point Roberts. The intertidal beaches with their ever- changing sandbars on a receding tide make an ideal resting and preening area for many shorebirds and *gulls* during the spring and fall migrations, always with the possibility of something unusual dropping in from the close proximity of the open waters off Point Roberts.

DIRECTIONS

From Highway 17 turn left at the lights for 56th Street (Point Roberts turnoff). Then turn left at 16th Avenue driving the 1 km (0.6 mi) to Beach Grove Road where another left turn will lead to Beach Grove Park and the school. Use the small parking lot for the local park to access some of the old back streets and the Beach Grove Park woodlot area.

To drive directly to the 15th Avenue dike continue on 56th Street to the 12th Avenue light at the shopping centre with another left turn onto 12th Avenue. A 0.7 km (0.4mi) drive past the golf course leads to the parking lot at the foot of 12 Avenue. The access to the dike walk is obvious from here.

For access to the farmland and Centennial Beach follow Boundary Bay Road to the right at the foot of 12th Avenue for 3.0 km (1.8 mi) to a T-junction turning left and following Centennial Parkway to a parking lot which accesses the beach, as well as the open savannah habitat to the north. It is possible to walk the beach, the dike or the trails inside of the dike between the two parking lots of 12th Avenue and Centennial Beach; there are also several public accesses to the shoreline between the houses of Beach Grove and Centennial Beach Communities.

Approximately one-third of the total area between Boundary Bay Road and the beach is Greater Vancouver Regional District park, which includes the dike and beach. Future plans for the area include the development of a multi-use wildlife habitat with freshwater ponds and marshes including all land east of the road.

BIRD SPECIES

The 12th Avenue dike walk has the advantage of permitting close observation of many *ducks, gulls*, shorebirds and some pelagic species under ideal conditions. The high tide brings the water literally up to the dike as well as slowly filling the lagoon.Winter populations of *ducks* in the bay exceed 70,000 with up to 18 species of mixed dabbling and diving *ducks,* 50,000 *Dunlin*, several hundred *Sanderling* are also winter residents. Add four *loon species, five grebe, three cormorant* and at least *six gull species* and a winter dike walk can be exciting.

With ducks and pelagic species arriving in early September and resident into April and May, the highlights to be looked for from this location are *Yellow-billed Loon, Clark's and Eared Grebes, Tufted Duck* and high numbers of *Eurasian Wigeon* (up to 23 individuals have been counted from this location).

The dike is a favoured preening area and resting beach for *Brant*. Very few *Brant* winter in the bay although the 1990-1992 wintering counts have improved with in excess of 200 birds seen at this location in late winter. The tidal effects on the bay create ideal feeding conditions for the non-migratory *Great Blue Heron* population and recent fall and winter counts from the 12th Avenue dike have reached 235 birds. The *Bald Eagle* winters locally and scavenges the tidelines of the bay feeding mainly on ducks and other water birds. Some 68 individuals have been seen here at one time, perched on drift logs or just standing on the beach, sometimes in small groups.

Over 20 raptor species are known to use the bay area primarily over the winter period. The dike walk at 12th Avenue, being typical habitat , is a good location to see *Peregine Falcon* and *Merlin* as they hunt over the saltwater and fields. *Prairie Falcon, Gyrfalcon* and *Northern Goshawk* may also appear as rare winter birds. Early morning or late evening walks have been successful in locating *Barn Owls,* probably from the nesting location at Beach Grove Park.

With the wintering flocks of *Dunlin* moving with the tide along this beach area an occasional *Western Sandpiper* or a more unusual wintering *Least Sandpiper* may be identified. The fall shorebird migration becomes apparent as early as the first week of July when adult *Western Sandpiper* begin to show up in the lagoon. In some years there is literally no clear break between the spring and fall shorebird migrations in this area. July, August and September are the active months for fall migrants with the numbers peaking in late August. With 50 species of shorebirds having been identified in the bay, this little corner will produce up to 25 species annually giving an observer the opportunity to study this rather difficult group of birds from relatively close range as they do not all follow the tideline each day, leaving representative birds resting and feeding in the small pools below the dike.

Western and Least Sandpipers are the most common shorebirds but all three *phalarope* and three species of *plover* have been seen inside the lagoon. *Stilt Sandpiper, Ruff, and Hudsonian Godwit* have turned up during fall migration but both of the *yellowlegs, dowitchers* and *Killdeer* make up the larger shorebirds during fall migration.

Spring shorebird migation from early April until mid May may not be as spectacular but most of the same species of birds will be seen in their more colourful breeding plumages.

The shallow lagoon and the long sloping shoreline outside of the sandbar seen from the pumphouse are excellent resting and preening areas for up to nine species of *gulls* throughout the year. August and September may bring in several *Franklin's Gull.* Up to 30 *Caspian Tern* including some very young birds have been seen since 1987. A few *Common Tern* pass as spring migrants and flocks of up to 150 may be seen in September either feeding or resting on the shoreline.

Inside the dike the summer birding is quiet with the predominant bird the *Savannah Sparrow, Cinnamon Teal, Mallard, Gadwall and Blue-winged Teal* all nest and single pairs of *Northern Harrier* and *Cooper's Hawk* nest regularly. The marsh is home to a good population of *Marsh Wren* and a few *Common Yellowthroat* and *Red-winged Blackbird* and possibly *Sora*. In winter look for an occasional *Swamp Sparrow* and a small flock of *Western Meadowlark.*

Spring and fall migration includes *Lincoln's Sparrow* and a good representation of *warblers,* with occasional *kingbirds* and *Northern Oriole*. Beach Grove Park seems to have good peak days during spring and fall migrations. May and September when relatively large numbers of insectivorous species may bunch up in this isolated woodlot.

With June being the month of least activity there are eleven months of excellent birding opportunities in the Boundary Bay area and with over 210 species recorded, this small area is very representative.

BOUNDARY BAY - 64TH TO 112TH STREET

Boundary Bay and the many birding sites within this region offer the best shorebirding in western Canada (at least 47 species, over 30 of them occurring regularly), much of Canada's best wintering raptor habitat (including all five North American falcons), large gull roosts and huge numbers of wintering waterfowl and other waterbirds. Its numerous hedgerows, woodlots, sloughs and fallow fields shelter and feed many migrant, wintering and resident passerine species. At least 75% of the species on the Vancouver Checklist, many of them vagrant, have been seen in the Boundary Bay area.

Boundary Bay is a large tidal bay about 16 km (9.9 mi) wide in an east-west direction, surrounded along its entire perimeter by a pedestrian-accessible dike. Its tidal sand and mudflats extend at low tide up to 2 km (1.2 mi) south of the dike, opening large feeding and roosting areas for waterfowl, gulls and shorebirds. The remnant saltmarsh forms a fringe between the high water mark and the dike. There are fairly extensive eelgrass beds at several locations offshore. As a general birding destination, Boundary Bay offers many excellent birding locations from Blackie Spit at the eastern end of the Bay to the Beach Grove Lagoon and Boundary Bay Regional Park in the west.

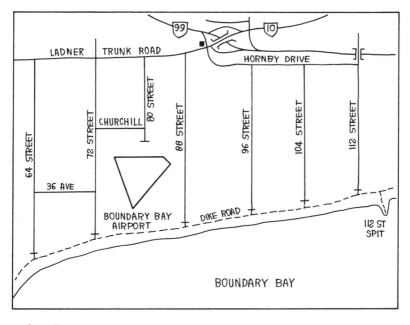

Boundary Bay

The entire length of the Bay has been diked to prevent high-tide damage and to drain the extensive natural salt-marshes to create farmland. Because the resulting agricultural lands surrounding the bay are fairly homogeneous, species accounts for any one of the numbered streets giving access to the Bay could, with little modification, stand for all. Other than agricultural use, commercial intrusion into the area is limited at present to a housing development and a big greenhouse on 64th Street, a small regional airport and a highly controversial golf course development on 72nd Street, and a smaller private air park at the south end of 104th Street. A raptor rehabilitation center is also on 72nd Street.

DIRECTIONS

General access to the Boundary Bay area is from Highway 99, the freeway between Vancouver and the U.S./Canada border, and/or Highway 10 (also called Ladner Trunk Road) and Hornby Drive. Highway 10 and Hornby Drive run east/west with north/south numbered streets 1.6 km. (1 mi.) apart. These streets run southward to the bay. Highway 10 is interrupted between 88th Street and 96th Street at the Mathews Exchange where Highway 10 meets the freeway (Highway 99). This interchange is a convenient shortcut for any approach except those from the Tsawwassen Ferry Terminal or Ladner.

Highway 10 parallels the freeway on its south side for 6.8 km (4.2 mi) from the Highway 17/Highway 10 junction to the Exchange, and angles up and over the freeway to the northeast. At the intersection of Highway 10 and Hornby Drive is a set of traffic lights. At this intersection is an R.C.M.P. detachment office on the southwest corner, and a firehall on the northeast corner. Hornby Drive begins here, initially going about 30 m south before curving left (east) to parallel the freeway, and ends at 112th Street. Once eastbound on Hornby, one reaches 96th, 104th and 112th Streets by turning right. When westbound on Highway 10, turn left to access 88th to 64th Streets.

Bus Access

Only two buses regularly serve this predominantly rural area and the stops are far apart. To reach the numbered streets along Highway 10 from downtown Vancouver, take the #604 South Delta bus to the Ladner Exchange and transfer to the #640 Scottsdale, an hourly eastbound bus which stops at several places along Highway 10, including the Mathews Exchange (westbound, this bus is called the #640 Tsawwassen Ferry.)

For direct access from downtown Vancouver to the Mathews Exchange, take the #351 Crescent Beach, which travels along the freeway. One can cross the freeway onto Hornby Drive via a pedestrian overpass just east of the Exchange.

BIRD SPECIES

64th Street

Coming from the west, turn right off Highway 10. Drive through the housing development for 0.8 km (0.5 mi). South of this point one enters agricultural land. Paralleling the street to the left are several sets of power lines and poles; *Red-tailed Hawk* and *Northern Harrier* use them for roosting and still-hunting perches. In winter and in passage, one can find *Rough-legged Hawk* and *Peregrine Falcon*. All five falcon species use this area in winter or in passage; only *Prairie Falcon* is irregular in the area. *Barn Owl* are relatively common throughout. (when checking barns, always ask permission of the property owners first.)

In spring and fall migrations, *Lesser Golden-Plovers* in small numbers, and *American Pipit* in far larger flocks use these fields. Wintering waterfowl use them as grazing lands, and shorebird flocks displaced by the bay's high tides await lower water in sometimes very large standing roosts. At the 3.8 km (2.4 mi) mark the railway right-of-way offers a slight rise from which to scan the surrounding fields, fenceposts and hedgerows for *Northern Shrike* and *Gyrfalcon*. The ditches along the tracks often contain waterfowl at any time of the year, but in spring and summer are home to nesting *Blue-winged and Cinnamon Teal.* A further 0.6 km (0.4 mi) leads to a

Great Blue Heron

large commercial greenhouse on the left where winter flocks of *Red-winged Blackbird, Brewer's Blackbird* and *European Starling* may occasionally harbour a *Yellow-headed Blackbird* or an even-rarer *Rusty Blackbird* (see also 96th St.) with a handful of overwintering *Brown-headed Cowbird*. At road's end check the hedgerows on either side, particularly good for mixed flocks of wintering and migrant sparrows such as *Golden-crowned, White-crowned, Savannah and Lincoln's Sparrows. American Tree, White-throated and Harris' Sparrows* are regular rarities in habitat such as this.

On the foreshore on an average winter day, one can see flocks of tens of thousands of ***Dunlin*** (sometimes mixed with a small proportion of ***Sanderling;*** a hard search may turn up one or two wintering ***Western Sandpipers***), huge numbers of ***American Wigeon*** and ***Green-winged Teal*** with smaller numbers of ***Northern Pintail*** and ***Mallard. Eurasian Wigeon*** are regular in these flocks, uncommon rather than rare, but the Eurasian race of the ***Green-winged Teal*** with its horizontal wingstripe is far scarcer. Early in the morning and late in the afternoon ***Short-eared Owl*** quarter the foreshore with the more common ***Northern Harriers,*** while ***Red-tailed and Rough-legged Hawks*** circle overhead. ***Bald Eagle*** are numerous, usually standing along the waterline. ***Peregrine*** regularly hunt along the foreshore, and ***Gyrfalcon*** (and, in recent winters, ***Prairie Falcon***) may appear here. In spring and fall there are large flocks of ***Black-bellied Plover*** and ***Western Sandpiper*** along the foreshore, usually tide-displaced from feeding areas at the eastern end of the bay. ***Northern Shrike*** are regular from October through April in small numbers. Examine any thickets along the dike for wintering and migrant passerines. Caution: the saltmarsh is fragile. Please stay on the obvious trails.

36th Avenue

This east-west road connects 64th and 72nd Streets 1.5 km (0.9 mi) south of Highway 10. Along its south side the plowed fields offer good habitat to both ***golden plovers, American Pipits, Lapland Longspurs*** and, more rarely, ***Snow Bunting***.

72nd Street

Coming from the west, turn right off Highway 10. Immediately south of Highway 10, hedgerows on both sides of the road offer good songbird habitat, and are productive all year. In winter, the fields beyond these hedgerows often contain large standing roosts of ***gulls*** sated from feeding in the Vancouver Landfill about 2 km (1.2 mi) to the north (gull enthusiasts take note: landfill management does not allow birding within the landfill), comprised of ***Glaucous-winged, Mew and Thayer's Gulls*** with ***Herring and California Gull*** in small numbers. ***Western and Glaucous Gulls*** are rare but regular. ***Ring-billed Gulls*** have become an abundant summer bird. These fields, extending south to the railway tracks, are also good raptor habitat. The trees adjacent to the road on the left side offer good raptor roosts and occasionally ***Long-eared Owl*** use them as a winter daytime roost.

The 72nd Street turf farms begin on the right side of the road just south of the railway. This location is Vancouver's likeliest for ***Buff-breasted Sandpiper, Lesser Golden-Plover, Baird's and Pectoral*** (and, rarely, ***Sharp-tailed) Sandpipers*** regularly use the farms, and ***Long-billed Curlew*** is vagrant here. Again, there is no public access: scan the area from roadside or the railway right-of-way which curves west around the back of the turf farms. Caution: coal trains using this railway move quickly in this location.

In winter, check the irrigation machinery for perched raptors, including **Snowy Owl.** South of the railway on the left side is the Boundary Bay Airport, another excellent wintering raptor area, particularly for **Rough-legged Hawk** and **Short-eared Owl.** Just south of the airport, about 2 km (1.2 mi) south of the highway on the left is the turn-off to the O.W.L. Rehabilitation Center where there are a number of non-releasable raptors on public display. A further 0.2 km (0.1 mi) on the left is a field where, in mid- to late April and early May, hundreds of **Black-bellied Plovers -** many in stunning breeding plumage - plus smaller numbers of other shorebird species gather at high tide to provide a spectacular and noisy display. Sometimes this flock contains small numbers of breeding -plumaged **Lesser Golden-Plover.**

Some 2.4 km (1.5 mi) south of Highway 10, on the left is the Benson Home, a heritage farmhouse, at the intersection of 72nd Street and 36th Avenue. Its gardens, fruit trees and surrounding hedgerows offer excellent cover for the large flocks of songbirds, particularly in winter. On the right is a farmyard which contains large wintering flocks of **Brewer's and Red-winged Blackbirds.** A large dead tree in this farmyard is the regular (and oft-contested) perch for the **Bald Eagle** and **Red-tailed Hawk,** and the

Dunlin

very occasional *Peregrine Falcon.* On the left for the next kilometer is a controversial golf-course project; the disturbed ground attracts migrant *pipits* and *Killdeer*. In the field to the right, a large radio/microwave tower provides a good raptor perch. At the end of the road are hedgerows often crowded with many wintering and migrant *sparrows.*

On the foreshore marsh and along the waterline, one can scan roosting shorebird and waterfowl flocks. About 1.5 km (0.9 mi) left along the dike is a thicket which often contains wintering *Yellow-rumped Warbler* with the more usual *sparrows*. Wintering *Western Meadowlark* and sometimes *Sandhill Crane* use the fields in this vicinity. The only remaining regularly-used foreshore site for the *Snowy Owl* (formerly more frequent along the foreshore before a saltmarsh regeneration program removed the great piles of driftwood logs they preferred) is about 1 km (0.6 mi) to the east of 72nd Street.

Boundary Bay Airport Access Road

Coming from the north, turn left off 72nd Street. A cross street just south of the railway linking 72nd and 80th Streets is shown on some maps as Churchill Street, dating back to W.W.II when the area contained a small settlement just north of the airport. There is pedestrian access over the railway at two locations 0.5 and 0.8 km (0.3-0.5 mi) east of 72nd Street respectively. This area consists of small abandoned orchard plots and gardens surrounded by crop and fallow fields providing excellent passerine and raptor habitat, with large gull (and occasionally shorebird) standing roosts. Potentially, one can see almost any raptor species in this area.

80th Street

Coming from the west, turn right off Highway 10. The only numbered street not reaching the Boundary Bay dike, 80th Street, terminates instead at the airport's eastern entrance. The fallow and marshy fields on either side are good *Northern Harrier* and open-country raptor habitat. The area near its southern end, with its familiar combination of ploughed and fallow fields surrounded by hedgerows and ditches so characteristic of the entire region, is most productive in fall and winter.

88th Street

Coming from the west, turn right off Highway 10. This is much like the other streets but with no obvious hotspots other than the gardens and other mixed habitats adjacent to farmhouses where wintering *finches* might gather, or the inevitable hedgerow/ditch combinations, especially at the road's end. In winter, check fenceposts for still-hunting raptors: both *Gyrfalcon* and *Prairie Falcon* have used these fields. Eastward from here, the high tide line moves progressively closer to the dike, squeezing the foreshore saltmarsh into an increasingly narrow fringe to 112th Street and making possible closer views of shorebirds and waterfowl.

96th Street

Coming from the west, turn right off Hornby Drive. 0.5 km (0.3 mi) south on the left is Cambridge Stables where large wintering *blackbird* and *European Starling* flocks gather, joined by the occasional *Yellow-headed Blackbird* and a few *Brown-headed Cowbird. Rusty Blackbird* has wintered here and may be regular. On the right a row of large conifers offer owl roost/raptor perch possibilities.

104th Street

Coming from the west, turn right off Hornby Drive. From the corner, large conifers and gardens on either side provide both good cover for songbirds and perches for raptors. A small woodlot and hedgerows at road's end may conceal the usual mixed flock of *sparrows* and, in migration, other passerines such as *warblers.*

The water line can reach very close to the dike at this point, making this a good location from which to scan waterfowl flocks and large groups of shorebirds displaced from their feeding areas to the east by rising tides.

112th Street

Coming from the west, turn right off Hornby Drive. Drive 0.6 km (0.4 mi) to road's end. When parking here, make sure to leave sufficient room around the driveways for large trucks and farm machinery to pass unobstructed: these are working farms. Check the fields for *Cattle Egret* in October and November. Once on the dike, one faces an old derelict cannery. To the immediate right is a modern pumphouse and drainage outflow. The grating over the outflow itself is often the fishing perch of *Green-backed Heron.* Many shorebirds use this area except at high tide: *Least, Western, and*

Long - billed Dowitcher

Semipalmated Sandpipers on the rocks, algal mats and floating debris bordering the channel; *Lesser and Greater Yellowlegs,* and sometimes *Solitary Sandpiper* on the muddy shores of the channel; *Black-bellied and Semipalmated Plovers* further out toward the tide line. *Loons, grebes* and diving *ducks* frequently come up the channel almost to the dike. To the left the dike is blocked by a low metal gate put there to prevent vehicle access. It is permissible to cross over this gate. Once across, one can scan a narrow loafing bar on the foreshore about 200 m (660 ft) east of the cannery where large concentrations of gulls, shorebirds and waterfowl gather (joined in summer by *Caspian Terns*).

It is from this point east that Boundary Bay offers some of the best shorebirding in Western Canada, particularly in the fall migration from late June until late October. In spring and fall migrations, one can see flocks of tens of thousands of *Western Sandpipers* staging through (a large proportion of the world's population) plus flocks of up to several thousand *Black-billed Plover*. It is in these flocks that one may locate many other species from *Long-billed Dowitcher* and *Semipalmated Plover* to "regular" rarities such as *Stilt Sandpiper* and *Hudsonian Godwit (Bar-tailed Godwit* has become almost regular in fall over the last few years), or accidentals such as *Snowy Plover, Little Stint* or Canada's first (and so far, only) *Far Eastern Curlew.* One of the best places on Boundary Bay to view these large gatherings is the head of a grassy spit almost 1 km (0.6 mi) east of the cannery. A trail diverges diagonally right from the dike 0.7 km (0.4 mi) from the cannery. From here one has an unobstructed view of Mud Bay, the main feeding ground.

Where there are shorebirds there are *falcons* to hunt them. Search the foreshore and the dead trees at the seaward edge of the woodlot just north of the grassy spit for perched *falcons*. Sometimes, *Sharp-shinned and Cooper's Hawks*, or roosting *Great -horned and Barn Owls* also use this woodlot, and it sometimes harbours good numbers of migrating passerines in spring. Transient *Ospreys* are regular here on the Bay, especially in fall. There are a few records of northbound *Golden Eagle* at the east end of the Bay.

Waterbirds here in summer include *Common Loon, Mallard, Gadwall,* and *White-winged and Surf Scoters.* Winter finds *Common and Red-throated Loons* with small numbers of *Pacific Loons* (far more numerous off Point Roberts to the southwest); *Horned, Western and Red-necked Grebes;* huge numbers of *American Wigeon, Northern Pintail, Green-winged Teal,* and *Mallard* inshore; great rafts of all three *scoter* species, *Oldsquaw, Common and Red-breasted Mergansers,* and both *scaup* species. *Pelagic and Double-crested Cormorants* are common. *Brant* feed in small numbers on eelgrass beds here, though their main staging area is further west off Beach Grove and Roberts Bank.

SERPENTINE FEN

Serpentine Fen is in Surrey some 50 km (31 mi) from downtown Vancouver on the way to the U.S. border. It is a triangular parcel of land covering approximately 100 ha (247 ac) sandwiched between Highways 99 and 99a, the Serpentine River, and the Nicomekl River.

This land was diked and drained around 1900. It was owned and farmed by the Stevenson family for many years. The huge barn, now in ruins, is all that remains of the farm. The farmland was purchased by the B.C. Department of Highways in 1961 during construction of Highway 99. The land is still owned by the Highways Ministry but since 1966 it has been administered by the B.C. Ministry of the Environment, Parks and Lands, Fish and Wildlife Branch.

Ducks Unlimited (Canada), together with the Wildlife Branch, built a system of ditches, dikes, freshwater marshes, ponds and islands. Ducks Unlimited has an office on the site. In 1973 the B.C. Government declared declared the fen to be a Wildlife Sanctuary.

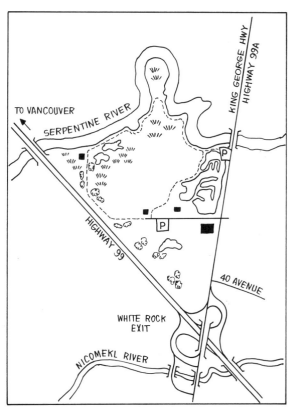

In 1972, Dr. Barry Leach of the Douglas College Institute of Environmental Studies began to operate an Environmental Study Centre at the fen which continued until 1977. During this period, Ducks Unlimited and the Wildlife Branch conducted a program designed to propagate a new *Canada Goose* population in the region. Also, ***pheasants*** were reared on the fen and released for shooting.

The White Rock and Surrey Naturalists' Society planted native

Serpentine Fen

trees and shrubs on the fen as a habitat improvement project between 1975 and 1983. In 1991 the Wildlife Branch removed the old south viewing tower and built a new one on the same spot. In 1992 a new tower was built on the dike near the saltmarsh. There are now three towers on the fen, the one on the West side having been constructed several years ago. The Wildlife Branch have also improved habitat by a program of ploughing and reseeding. Serpentine fen is not yet designated a Wildlife Management Area.

The Serpentine Fen lies in the floodplain of the Serpentine and Nicomekl Rivers and is very close to the ocean at Mud Bay. The rivers are tidal where they run through the fen and are diked for several miles. There are few large trees on the fen but some of the area is covered in bushes such as elderberry, hawthorn and hardhack, and also brambles and small trees - mostly Pacific crabapple. The open part of the fen consists of some hay fields, ponds and ditches bordered by bulrushes and sedges. The water level is controlled by floodgates. In summer much water is diverted to nearby farms for irrigation.

DIRECTIONS

The fen can be reached from Vancouver either by the Highway 99 or by Highway 99a (the King George Highway). If approaching from Highway 99 it is best to take the White Rock exit and then the right fork which says "Crescent Beach". This road goes over a one way bridge over the Nicomekl River and comes out on Crescent Road. Turn left here and follow to the traffic lights at the King George Highway. Turn left again keeping in the left lane and follow the King George Highway north to the Serpentine River. Park here near the bridge. There is also a parking lot on 44 Avenue, but it is not recommended. There are covered picnic tables at this lot, but there are no public toilets at the fen.

BIRD SPECIES

Birding at the fen, like many other places, is best in spring, fall and winter. Much depends on the water levels. High levels good for the ducks, lower levels with muddy edges good for shorebirds. Winter can be good here if the ponds are not frozen.

Leaving your car parked on the west side of the highway walk along the dike on the south side of the Serpentine river. To the south along the highway there is a fairly large body of water which stretches to 44 Avenue. Most of the birds on this pond tend to stay near the highway side but do not try viewing from the road shoulders. Some of the paths are posted "no public access." Please observe this rule to protect the birds. This pond supports nearly all the species of dabbling *ducks* normally found in the area. Also present are *scaup, Common Goldeneye, Bufflehead, Common and Hooded Mergan-*

sers, Canada Geese and occasionally a *Snow Goose* or a *White-fronted Goose. Tundra Swans* and a *White Pelican* have visited. When there are muddy edges *Greater and Lesser Yellowlegs, dowitchers*, and *Pectoral Sandpiper* are usually seen and the fen has been host to *Solitary, Sharp-tailed and Buff-breasted Sandpipers, Ruff and* even *Spotted Redshank.*

To start your walk follow the dike along the south bank of the Serpentine river. It is tidal in this area. Found here are *Horned, Red-necked and Western Grebes*. Also seen with some luck are *Clark's Grebe*, and *Common, Red-throated* and perhaps *Pacific Loon. Common and Red-breasted Mergansers* are usually on the river and *Belted Kingfishers* and sometimes *Common or Caspian Terns* can be seen from the dikes. *Double-crested Cormorants* sit on the pilings and *Spotted Sandpipers* follow the dike banks.

A short walk west along the dike brings a bend to the north and with it a good view of the left side of the dike. This area is known as the long meadow. It sometimes has ponds and other times it is almost dry. It has been home to many dabbling ducks, and *Red-necked and Wilson's Phalaropes. American Avocet* has nested here and *Black-necked Stilt* has been seen.

Tundra Swan

From here the river follows a winding course at one spot some distance from the dike. At this bend there is a stand of small trees and bushes where *American Tree Sparrow* and *Common Redpoll* have visited in winter along with *Northern Shrike* and *Mountain Chickadee.* There is a saltwater marsh at this bend where *Killdeer* and *Green-winged Teal* are usually present. One of the three viewing towers at the fen is located here. As you walk the dikes you will hardly ever (in season) be out of sight or sound of the *Marsh Wren* and *Common Yellowthroat.*

As you approach the west end of the fen the path turns south and you will see the second tower. This gives a good overview of the area and is a good place to spot the first *swallows* of the year, usually near the end of February. There are ponds here which are good in the wet season for *Blue-winged and Cinnamon Teal* in spring. *Sora* and *Virginia Rail* have occasionally been seen.

The path continues south until it meets what used to be 44th Avenue, now cut off by the freeway. Here we have a few hundred meters of road with Pacific crabapples, hawthorns and elderberries providing food and shelter for a variety of songbirds. On the south side of the road are hay fields good for **Savannah Sparrow**. The hedges are good habitat for **House and Purple Finches, Rufous-sided Towhee, Bewick's Wren, American Robin, Cedar Waxwing, Bushtit, Steller's Jay, Evening Grosbeak, Rufous Hummingbird** and **Willow Flycatcher**. Sparrows to be found include **White-crowned and Golden-crowned** as well **Fox and Song** and once or twice a **Harris'** has appeared. **Warblers** to be encountered are mostly **Orange-crowned, Yellow and Yellow-rumped** with an occasional **Wilson's**.

Swallow boxes line the road with nesting **Tree and Violet-green Swallows**. Also present are **Cliff, Barn** (nesting around the buildings), some **Northern Rough-winged** and the occasional **Bank Swallow**. **Mourning Doves** sit on the wires along with the **Red-winged and Brewer's Blackbirds**. The **Ring-necked Pheasant** may call from the fields.

There is another viewing tower part way down the road and the path leads past this tower. Before going on this path it is a good idea to continue down the road to view the rest of the shrubbery. Some of the rarer *sparrows* have been seen here. **Warblers** are found in the fruit trees around the Ducks Unlimited office. **Black-headed Grosbeak** and **Eastern Kingbird** have been seen in this spot.

Throughout the fen you can see **Great Blue Heron** and sometimes a **Green-backed Heron** or **American Bittern** hiding along a ditch. **Cattle Egret** and **Great Egret** have also visited. Overhead can be busy too with **Northern Harrier** and **Red-tailed Hawk** nearly always present. The **Rough-legged Hawk** appears in late fall. Also possible are **Merlin, American Kestrel** and even **Peregrine Falcon**. Once or twice a **Gyrfalcon** has been noted. **Cooper's and Sharp-shinned Hawks** are sometimes seen. **Short-eared Owl** does occur but not as much as previously. In winter the odd **Snowy Owl** will drop in. **Bald Eagles** are quite common and once in a while, a **Golden Eagle** will fly overhead. **Osprey** have been seen over the river. Seven species of *gulls* are present at various times and an occasional **Black Tern** visits the ponds.

The round trip through the fen takes about an hour and a half depending on how much stopping is done.

Peregrine Falcon

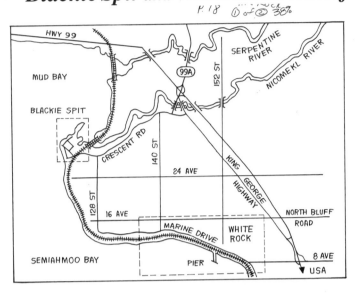

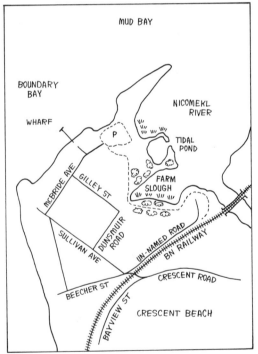

Blackie Spit and White Rock and South Surrey

BLACKIE SPIT AND
WHITE ROCK WATERFRONT

The Semiahmoo (sem-ee-ah-moo) Peninsula is the southwest part of Surrey. The peninsula is bounded to the west by Mud Bay and Boundary Bay, and to the south by Semiahmoo Bay.

5,000 years ago, the peninsula was inhabited by Coast Salish peoples. When Captain George Vancouver anchored the "Discovery" in the bay in 1792, a populous village of the Semiahmoo band flourished at the mouth of the river which empties into the bay just north of the present day international boundary. Members of the band still live on the Semiahmoo Indian Reserve at the mouth of the Campbell River. A large boulder, a relic of the Ice Age on White Rock's East Beach, was used as a navigation aid. The rock, limed white with guano, eventually gave the city its name.

European settlement began in the mid-1800's. By 1910, White Rock was being promoted as a resort area because of its mild climate and sandy beaches. A cottage community sprang up along the Semiahmoo Bay waterfront. The City of White Rock encompasses almost 8 square km (3 square miles), and is surrounded by the southern portion of Surrey. Most of the land on the peninsula has been developed for residential use.

Blackie Spit (once an Indian encampment) was settled by Walter Blackie in 1871. He farmed the land on which the community of Crescent Beach is now situated. Today, Blackie Spit refers to the sandy point jutting into Mud Bay (the shallow northeastern part of Boundary Bay), at the mouth of the Nicomekl River and adjacent undeveloped land.

The vegetation here consists of various grasses and shrubs, Himalayan blackberry, and glasswort in the saltwater marsh areas, with a scattering of trees around the tidal pond and Farm Slough. Birding the Blackie Spit area is best during migration periods and in winter, although rarities can show up in any season.

DIRECTIONS

To reach Blackie Spit from Vancouver (about 30 km (18.6 mi) from downtown), take Highway 99 south, past Mud Bay, and take the White Rock/Crescent Beach exit onto Highway 99A (King George Highway). On 99A, turn right (west) at the first traffic light onto Crescent Road. About 5 km (3.1 mi) from 99A, Crescent Road drops down a hill and crosses a railroad track. At a V-intersection just beyond the tracks, bear right onto Sullivan Street. Turn right again onto McBride Avenue, the last road before the beach. The parking area is at the north end of McBride, but is open only from 8:00 a.m. to dusk: if you arrive before 8:00 a.m., park outside and walk in. Another place with room to park a few cars is on Dunsmuir Avenue, off Sullivan. This is the closest access point to "Farm Slough".

Blackie Spit can also be reached by the Crescent Beach bus (#351), which provides service from Vancouver to Sullivan and McBride. Service is every half-hour on weekdays, and hourly during evenings, weekdays, and holidays.

BIRD SPECIES

Tide levels are important when looking for waterbirds and shorebirds. If you do not have a copy of Canadian Tide and Current Tables published annually by Fisheries and Oceans Canada, check the Peace Arch News or Vancouver newspapers for tide tables. Tidal fluctuations in Mud Bay and Boundary Bay are large, from as little as 1.8 m (6 ft) to as much as 4.3 m (14 ft) within a 24-hour period. Daily high tides vary from about 4.0 m (13 ft) to 4.9 m (16 ft). Waterfowl are best seen during moderately high tides of 3.7 m (12 ft) and higher. Shorebirds are generally best seen during tides of about 3.0 m (10 ft) to 3.8 m (12.5 ft). During lower tides, there is so much exposed mud and sand that the birds range over an enormous area. High tides push the birds nearer shore where they can be easily seen. On the other hand, maximum tides of 4.6 m (15 ft) or more force the birds to other areas, such as the inaccessible east shore of Mud Bay. Plan to arrive at least an hour before the expected optimum viewing time; the water moves in surprisingly fast.

Walk Blackie Spit proper, through the growth in the centre, as well as both shores. Migrant *Lapland Longspur* (September-October) and *Snow Bunting* (November-December) are sometimes seen. Watch for *Dunlin, Sanderling,* and *Black-bellied Plover* from fall through late spring. Scan the *loons, grebes, gulls,* and waterfowl offshore. *Black Brant* are sometimes seen, especially in spring.

The saltwater marsh across the Nicomekl River mouth, opposite Blackie Spit, is used by loafing *gulls* and *Great Blue Heron* at high tide, and may at times teem with shorebirds. Harbour seals haul out regularly on certain islets. There is no public access to this area; view it by telescope from Blackie Spit. Do NOT attempt to cross on the railway trestle.

The shallow, sheltered waters off the east side of the spit are attractive to wintering dabbling ducks. Look for *Eurasian Wigeon,* and occasionally the Eurasian race of *Green-winged Teal,* among the other ducks. Shorebirds and *gulls* like to rest in the small saltwater marsh along the east side of the spit. The common *gulls* are *Glaucous-winged* (resident), *Mew* (winter), and *Ring-billed* (summer). In fall look for the rare *Franklin's Gull* among the flocks of *Bonaparte's*. The *California Gull* is a spring and fall migrant. In winter, look for a *Herring Gull* among the *Thayer's*. Watch for

Caspian Tern (May-September) and ***Common Tern*** (August - September).

Farther south along the east side of Blackie Spit is a small tidal pond, surrounded by small trees which attract ***sparrows*** and ***finches*** in winter and ***warblers*** in spring and fall. At low tide, it is possible to continue walking along the shore, across the narrow channel which drains the pond, but at high tide, you may have to detour around the west side of the pond. In either case, after crossing an open, sandy area, you will reach "Farm Slough", a shallow backwater of the Nicomekl River at the southeastern corner of Blackie Spit. At the optimal tidal levels (about 11 feet to 13 feet), this sheltered slough is often full of shorebirds and ***ducks.*** One of the best viewing spots is on the north side of the slough's mouth, marked by a row of low pilings, remnants of a bygone oyster cannery. From this point, behind a sheltering screen of broom, one may scan both Farm Slough and the adjacent Nicomekl estuary.

Sanderling

Summer and early fall produces the greatest variety of shorebirds, but some species are present all year. Small flocks of ***Greater Yellowlegs*** and ***Long-billed Dowitcher*** can usually be found in winter. A few non-breeding ***Whimbrel*** may linger in the vicinity all summer. A few ***Semipalmated Sandpiper*** may be found in late summer among the abundant ***Western Sandpiper.*** Such locally-rare shorebirds as ***Willet, Hudsonian Godwit, Marbled Godwit,*** and ***Long-billed Curlew*** have all been seen here on a number of occasions.

On the south side of "Farm Slough", a path leads along the wooded dike bordering the slough .This is a good area for passerines. It joins the jogging trail on a parallel dike on the southern side of the slough's mouth. Turning right (southwest), walk along an unnamed road which parallels the railroad tracks on the far side of the Dunsmuir farm. Scan the field for **Northern Shrike** in winter. The road is lined by tall Lombardy poplars, which may harbour **Northern Oriole,** and by dense shrub thickets. Watch the tall trees up the hillside, and listen for **Pileated Woodpecker, Band-tailed Pigeon,** and **Steller's Jay.**

Washrooms, open all year from 8:00 a.m. to sundown, are located at the foot of Beecher Avenue in Crescent Beach. The White Rock and Surrey Naturalists operate an information centre here on weekends from 1:00 to 5:00 p.m., October through May, and a bird checklist for Blackie Spit is available.

White Rock Waterfront

The City of White Rock has developed a promenade 2.2 km (1.4 mi) long, with parking areas, along the East and West beaches. The two beaches are divided by the pier, which extends almost 500 m (1,650 ft) southward into Semiahmoo Bay.

DIRECTIONS

To reach the White Rock waterfront from Highway 99, take the 8th Avenue exit onto Highway 99A, then turn right (west) onto 8th Avenue. After several blocks, 8th Avenue becomes Marine Drive. Parking lots are located at frequent intervals along the Drive (there may be a fee).

BIRD SPECIES

Winter is the best time to look for birds in the waters of the bay, when large numbers of wintering waterfowl are present. Therefore, the following comments pertain to that season. A telescope is recommended. View from the promenade, and from the pier. Depending on the tide (mid- to high-tide is best), the wind (and other variables known only to birds), **loons, grebes,** and **ducks** may be plentiful. Scrutinize the rock breakwater at the end of the pier for **Black Turnstone.** Watch for **Bald Eagle** overhead.

Common Loon are easily found. **Red-throated Loon** are considered uncommon, and **Pacific Loon** are uncommon to rare. **Yellow-billed Loon** are very rare.

Western and Horned Grebe are common, while **Red-necked Grebe** is fairly common. Look carefully for **Eared Grebe**; one or more winter in the bay nearly every year. The

Eared Grebe may not associate with other grebe species. Common wintering ducks include *Mallard* (resident), *Northern Pintail, American Wigeon, Greater and Lesser Scaup, Common and Barrow's Goldeneye, Bufflehead,* all three *scoter* species, and *Ruddy Duck. Harlequin Duck, Oldsquaw,* and *mergansers* are less common. These and alcids usually prefer the deeper water and rocky off-shore terrain west of the pier and the West Beach. *Common Murre, Marbled Murrelet,* and *Pigeon Guillemot* are uncommon.

An assortment of *gulls*, mostly *Glaucous-winged, Mew, and Ring-billed,* loiter about the pier and beaches, alert for handouts. Look them over for *Thayer's* and perhaps *Herring Gull.* Most of the adult *Glaucous-winged Gull* show darker wing tips, indicative of hybridization with *Western Gull.*

Shorebirds such as *Black Turnstone, Dunlin,* and *Sanderling* are sometimes seen in suitable habitat, or flying by.

A short distance inland from Marine Drive's commercial strip, and westward from West Beach, the terrain rises rather steeply to 61 m (201 ft).

By walking along the Burlington Northern Railroad tracks (watch out for trains!) below the bluff, it is possible to cover the entire rocky waterfront from White Rock to Crescent Beach. The distance from the White Rock pier to Crescent Beach is about 8.5 km (5.3 mi) so allow 4-5 hours. At two locations, a wooden staircase provides access to the residential streets on the bluffs above. These are the "1001" steps at the west end of 15A Avenue, and a similar set of steps at the west end of 24th Avenue.

Western Grebe

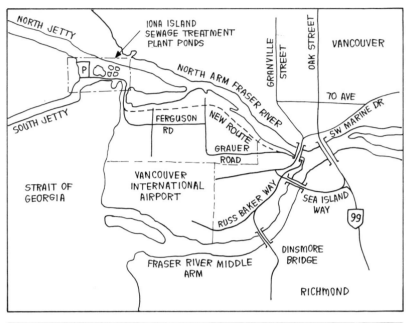

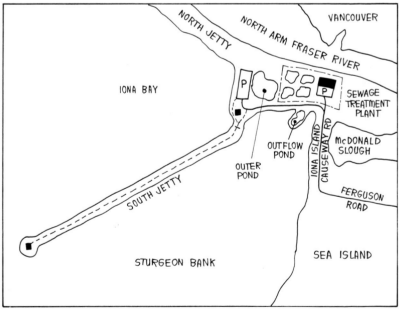

Lulu Island and Iona Island

IONA ISLAND

Iona Island, one of the west coast's premiere birding areas, owes its fame to a sewage treatment plant. Prior to 1958, the island was accessible only by boat. The sewage plant's discharge pipe, the 4 km ((2.5 mi) long South Jetty was completed in 1988. The Greater Vancouver Regional District Parks Department now oversees the public areas of the island and has ambitious plans for the North Jetty which is presently off limits. A habitat restoration project is underway in the area between the sewage ponds and the jetties. It is hoped that the riparian and pond edge plantings will provide breeding habitat for the *Yellow-headed Blackbird* which are expected to be displaced from nearby Sea Island by an airport expansion. Although this chapter is concerned primarily with the South Jetty and the sewage lagoons, the ponds and planted area in between have already hosted an impressive number of species. As with most urban parks, sunny weekends bring out the crowds. If the jetty is busy, visit the sewage ponds. Only birders are allowed here, and you can still scan the public ponds from the private side of the fence. Iona Island is a world class place to see shorebirds and pelagic birds from land, and is only 30 minutes from downtown Vancouver.

DIRECTIONS

There are numerous ways of getting to Iona Regional Park. The following are the most direct routes. 1) When going to Iona from Vancouver, get on Oak Street and follow it south over the Oak Street Bridge. Take the very first exit off the bridge and stay on that road through three traffic lights and over a small lift bridge. 2) If coming from the south on Highway 99, or from the east on Highway 91, follow the signs for Vancouver International Airport and watch for the small lift bridge. After crossing this narrow green bridge, follow the signs for Iona by taking the first right after the bridge. In the field to the left and along the powerlines watch for *Crested Myna*. The road soon bends left and becomes Grauer Road. Please note that the access from Grauer Road will soon be changed due to the construction of a third runway at Vancouver International Airport.

This is a great place for raptors and waterfowl in the winter. *Greater White-fronted Goose* and *Eurasian Wigeon* are regularly seen among the large flocks of *Canada Goose* and *American Wigeon. Short-eared Owl* and *Northern Shrike* are also present throughout the winter. The road bends right and becomes MacDonald Road which should be followed for 500 m (1,650 ft), where Ferguson Road crosses. Turn left here and continue watching for raptors. Ferguson Road bends right and takes you along a short causeway onto Iona Island. When on the causeway check both to the left and to the right for shorebirds, *terns, gulls,* and *ducks.* As you drive onto the island you will see the sewage plant straight ahead. Veer left before the plant and note the large orange gate. Just beyond this gate, on the right is the birder's gate to the sewage lagoons, and on the left side of the road is the old sewage outflow pond. The jetty, beach, and park ponds are just up the road at the parking lot.

South Jetty

Vancouver's sewage, after treatment, is deposited over 4 km offshore into the Strait of Georgia. Happily for birders the means of transport is a sea level jetty with an observation area at the far end. There is a semi-paved road that makes bicycling an attractive alternative to an 8 km (5 mi) round trip on foot. Motorized vehicles are prohibited on the jetty. Except for a portable washroom, the jetty has absolutely no facilities. The weather can change very quickly, and visitors are advised to carry warm clothing, water, and a snack.

Probably the most important consideration when visiting Iona Island is the tide level, followed by the season. At low tide in the summer the jetty will provide great views of *Green-winged Teal* dabbling in the mud, and not much else. Always time your visit with a rising tide. The summer months are generally the least active time for the jetty. The seabirds and waterfowl are on their breeding grounds and will not return until fall. The bright spot in this otherwise quiet season is the chance of seeing *Wandering Tattler.* The last of the jetty and the rocky breakwater at the very end are probably the best areas in Vancouver for finding this much wanted bird. Sightings exist from late July to the end of September, with most reports from mid to late August. Other shorebirds will rest along the jetty at high tide.

From July to September large numbers of *Western Sandpipers* and some *Least, Semipalmated, Baird's, and Pectoral Sandpipers* may be seen. The autumn brings returning waterfowl and seabirds. Migrating *Bonaparte's Gull* and *Common Tern* will draw *Parasitic Jaeger. Snow Geese* roost to the south along the Sea Island shoreline. *Thayer's and Mew Gulls* return for the winter, as do flocks of *Dunlin* and occasional *Black-bellied Plover. Lapland Longspur* are fairly regular in September and October, and by late November there is usually a small flock of *Snow Bunting* moving along the jetty.

Mid-fall to early spring is when the South Jetty is in its glory. *Common, Pacific and Red-throated Loons, Western, Red-necked and Horned Grebes, Double-crested, Pelagic and Brandt's Cormorants, Great Blue Heron, Snow and Canada Goose, Mallard, Gadwall, Green-winged Teal, American Wigeon, Northern Pintail, Northern Shoveller, Ruddy Duck, Canvasback, Greater and Lesser Scaup, Black, White-winged and Surf Scoter, Oldsquaw, Barrow's and Common Goldeneye, Bufflehead, Red-breasted Merganser, Black-bellied Plover, Dunlin, and Mew, Ring-billed, California, Herring, Thayer's, and Glaucous-winged Gulls* can all be found from the jetty with little difficulty. Rarer, but regularly seen and to be looked for species include *Clark's and Eared Grebe, Greater White-fronted Goose, Brant, Eurasian Wigeon, Redhead, Ring-necked Duck, Tufted Duck, Harlequin Duck, Common Merganser, Black Turnstone, Surfbird, Black Oystercatcher, Rock Sandpiper, Wandering*

Tattler, Western Gull, Glaucous Gull, Pigeon Guillemot, Common Murre, Marbled Murrelet and *Rhinoceros Auklet.*

Although birding from the jetty is great all winter, the chance of seeing true rarities increases dramatically either during or just after a storm system. Records exist for *Sooty Shearwater, King Eider, Little, Common Black-headed and Sabine's Gulls,* and *Black-legged Kittiwake.* The passing of a storm front usually precedes such sightings.

Iona Island supports a sizeable number of raptors throughout the winter. *Northern Harriers* and *Short-eared Owls* work the shoreline marshes. *Bald Eagles* cull the injured and unwary ducks and gulls. A *Snowy Owl* may also be seen.

Iona Island's South Jetty has the ability to bring offshore waters, and their associated birds within reach. It can also bring the vagaries of coastal weather. A spotting scope, though not absolutely necessary, will be appreciated when scanning that distant flock of *scaup,* looking for the elusive *Tufted Duck.*

Sewage Ponds

The good folks that run the sewage treatment plant and adjacent ponds are very tolerant of birders. So tolerant in fact, that they have installed a locking gate solely for our use. The plant management ask that we park on the roadside near the gate, rather than using their parking lot and risk having vehicles locked in for the night. To obtain a key to the plant gate, call the names given at the end of the Bird Alert tape (737-9910). The levels of the four sewage ponds are controlled according to the demands of the plant. During the height of shorebird migration at least one pond is kept at an ideal level. Another pond will likely have one year's worth of vegetation, and hosts breeding *Sora* and possibly *Wilson's Phalarope.* The shrubs around the perimeter of the ponds attract a good variety of passerines during migration. The sewage ponds are best known for their shorebirds - thousands of "peeps", a good variety of species, and the chance of an ultra-rarity.

When planning a trip to the sewage ponds, be sure your visit coincides with a rising tide. As the birds are pushed off the diminishing mudflats, they crowd into the sewage ponds. The first shorebirds generally appear in April and numbers peak by mid-May. By the end of June a few northbound stragglers meet the vanguard of returning adults.

The common spring shorebirds are *Western Sandpiper,* both *dowitchers, Black-bellied Plover, Semipalmated Plover, Killdeer, Dunlin,* and both *Greater and Lesser Yellowlegs.* Less common, but seen every spring are *Semipalmated and Least Sandpipers, Lesser Golden- Plovers, Pectoral Sandpiper,* and *Baird's Sandpiper.*

Spring migration is fast and purposeful, unlike fall with its more leisurely pace. The returning shorebird numbers build up through July and increase dramatically by the end of the month with the arrival of the juveniles. Every high tide from late July through early September will find thousands of birds crowded into the ponds. The gravel path around each pond allows for very close looks and is ideal for photography. Some species appear quite tame and will approach to a distance that tests your binocular's close focus capabilities. The vast number of shorebirds attract *Peregrine Falcon* and *Merlin*. The adults will deftly pluck a *sandpiper* from the swirling flock, while the young *falcons* learn the hard and often hilarious way. The newly created islands in the Outer Pond also attract large numbers of shorebirds, which can best be viewed from the sewage ponds side of the fence. Through September, the number of small *sandpipers* diminish, and the ponds now hold smaller flocks of *yellowlegs, dowitchers, Pectoral and Baird's Sandpipers.* September and October are the time to carefully scan the *Pectoral Sandpiper* for the rare but regularly occurring *Sharp-tailed Sandpiper.* Iona Island is arguably the most reliable site in Canada for this species, and when present, can be viewed from within 10 m (33 ft). By mid-October the *Dunlin* have arrived, and with a very few *Black-bellied Plover, Western Sandpiper, Greater Yellowlegs,* and *Long-billed Dowitcher* make up the winter shorebird population.

In addition to the species mentioned, the following shorebirds are seen at least annually at the sewage ponds; *Red-necked Phalarope, Solitary and Stilt Sandpipers, Ruff, Common Snipe, Red Knot* and *Sanderling.* Iona's most famous visitor was a *Spoonbill Sandpiper* that showed up in late July, 1978, and stayed around long enough to be seen by hundreds of ecstatic birders. Not in the same league, but certainly contributing to Iona's legendary status are the following "Casual Accidental" shorebird sightings: *American Avocet, Snowy Plover, Curlew and White-rumped Sandpipers, Rufous-necked and Little Stints, Upland Sandpiper*, and *Red Phalarope.*

Although the sewage ponds have an enviable reputation amongst birding hotspots, that reputation goes beyond shorebirds. All six species of *swallows* can be found here, large flocks of *American Pipit* pass through, *Vaux's and Black Swifts* are seen in approaching storm clouds and three species of teal breed in the ponds. Some of the more exciting non-shorebird finds over the years include *Garganey, Ross' Goose, Common Moorhen, Yellow Wagtail, Purple Martin, Say's Phoebe, Lazuli Bunting, Loggerhead Shrike, Tropical Kingbird, Ash-throated, Least and Alder Flycatchers, Northern Mockingbird, Sage Thrasher, Common Grackle, and Brewer's, Grasshopper* and *Harris' Sparrow.*

From offshore alcids to the fine points of shorebird plumages, winter "dickeybirding" to unravelling the mystery of gulls - no matter what your birding interests, Iona Island holds the promise of good, and the possibility of exceptional birding.

LULU ISLAND

The City of Richmond encompasses almost 20 islands, the largest by far being Lulu Island. Here between the North, Middle and South Arms of the Fraser River is concentrated much of Richmond's industry and almost all of its residential area. It is no surprise, therefore, that for birders Lulu Island is eclipsed in its popularity by its sisters Sea Island and Iona Island. But while these two islands can lay claim to many rare sightings, Lulu Island provides a greater variety of habitats and offers the opportunity to see a large cross-section of the birds of the Lower Mainland.

A sub-tropical climate encouraged the growth of dense broad-leaf forest which, over time, was replaced by coastal swamp and cedar forest cover. Glaciation followed, only to recede leaving a hugh plain that has evolved into the delta of today. One quarter of Richmond's 110 square km (40 square mi) lies 5.1 m (17 ft) above sea level, the remaining land at 1.2-2.1 m (4-7 ft). Sloughs crisscross the agricultural land creating a haven for many species of waterfowl while the remaining cottonwood and crabapple stands (which once grew all across Lulu Island), provide a refuge for many species of landbirds.

While all of the birding areas of Lulu Island are easily reached by car, the development of recreational facilities has provided an extensive network of trails that prohibit vehicular traffic; a boon for the birder who enjoys walking or biking. The North,

Wandering Tattler

Middle and South Arms of the Fraser River provide open water that have good concentrations of *loons, grebes, ducks* and *geese* from late autumn until early spring. Sturgeon Bank, running the length of the west side of the island, provides a year-round marsh habitat for *ducks* and migrating shorebirds. The inland trail, Shell Road, runs through fields of blueberries that thrive on the peat bog; small stands of spruce, cedar, cottonwood and willow abound.

The Middle Arm of the Fraser River can be explored in its entire length from a dike, or seawall, that runs from just south of the Sea Island Bridge to Terra Nova in the northwest corner of Lulu Island.

DIRECTIONS

Lulu Island is bisected by Highway 99 connecting Vancouver to the north, and Delta to the south. From Vancouver, Oak Street and the Oak Street Bridge carry traffic into central Richmond. Granville Street and the Arthur Laing Bridge lead onto Sea Island from which the Dinsmore and Sea Island Bridges both connect to Lulu Island. Traffic from Vancouver can also take the Knight Street Bridge across the North Fraser River. From the south, Highway 99 runs through the George Massey Tunnel bringing traffic from the United States border, the ferry terminal at Tsawwassen, Delta and White Rock. Highway 91 connects Highway 99 to the Alex Fraser Bridge for traffic from Surrey and to New Westminster by way of the Westminster Highway and the Queensborough Bridge.

BIRD SPECIES

River Road parallels the dike for 5.0 km (3.1 mi) to its ending at Terra Nova. For those that combine birding and biking this is a good starting point for a 23 km (14.3 mi) round trip to the fishing port of Steveston. The best birding on this stretch of the river is usually to the west of the Dinsmore Bridge. There are a number of places to park a vehicle between the bridge and Terra Nova. *Great Blue Heron* is common along the length of the dike and *Canada Goose* can be seen at most times. Scan flocks in autumn and winter for *Greater White-fronted Goose*. In summer watch for the distinctively stiff flight of *Spotted Sandpiper*; these nest on the opposite bank of the river. Check the driftwood in the River, because quite often what seems to be lumber turns out to be the head of a harbour seal.

From October to April there are large numbers of *Mallard* and *American Wigeon* close to the seawall. Watch for *Gadwall, Green-winged Teal* and *Scaup* amongst them. Check the *wigeon* closely because there are always several *Eurasian* to be found. Common sightings further out are *Red-breasted Merganser, Surf Scoter, Bufflehead,*

Common Goldeneye, Ruddy Duck, Red-throated and Common Loons, plus *Western and Red-necked Grebes.* Less often seen in the river are *Oldsquaw, Barrow's Goldeneye* and *Common Merganser.* Check the grebes close to shore; *Pied-billed and Horned Grebes* are common and *Eared Grebe* can occasionally be seen.

Midway between the Dinsmore Bridge and Terra Nova a small marsh has been reconstructed by the City of Richmond where *Red-winged Blackbird* abounds. Check for *Common Snipe* in this area and across the river for wintering *Double-crested and Pelagic Cormorants.* Close to Terra Nova watch for the remains of the old cannery constructed in 1892 and taken down in 1978. This marks the beginning of the Sturgeon Bank marshes; *Canvasback, Northern Shoveler* and *American Coot* are often seen from the parking areas. *Red-throated Loon* frequents the river in winter and the *Yellow-billed Loon* has been seen with them.

Sturgeon Bank and the western edge of Lulu Island can be explored from the seawall that runs 5.5 km (3.4 mi) south from Terra Nova to Garry Point Park and Steveston. Road access to the seawall is limited along its length; five streets provide intermediate points of entry. To reach these from Terra Nova head back along River Road for 1.4 km (0.9 mi) to No. 1 Road, turn right heading south and turn right on any of the following: Westminster Highway, Blundell Road, Francis Road, Williams Road or Steveston Highway.

Bald Eagles have nested in trees of Terra Nova mid-way between the two parking areas. Recently residential development has taken over much of what was some of the best agricultural land in the Lower Mainland. Public pressure restricted urban growth but you need to walk south along the seawall for about 1.0 km (0.6 mi), past the end of Westminster Highway, to appreciate the land as it was. *Ring-necked Pheasant* thrives in the fields while *Red-tailed Hawk, Northern Harrier* and *Short-eared Owl* can be seen for most of the year. These are joined in winter by *Rough-legged Hawk.* Check ditches in late spring and summer for *Killdeer,* often with young, *Cinnamon and Blue-winged Teal* and, during migration periods, check for *yellowlegs* and *dowitchers.*

The marsh to the west runs the length of the seawall. In fall and spring the sounds of *Snow Geese* fill the air as they gather for migration. *Northern Pintail* live year round while *Trumpeter and Tundra Swans* spend the winter here. *American Bittern, Sora* and *Virginia Rail* are secretive inhabitants while *Barn Owl, Long-eared Owl* and *Peregrine Falcon* can be seen hunting. Uncommon visitors to the area, such as the *Cattle Egret,* have also been seen in the marsh.

At the south end of the seawall is Garry Point Park where *Brewer's Blackbird* and *Brown-headed Cowbird* occur most of the year and can be found here in the winter months along with the **Northwestern Crow** and the occasional **Common Raven.** To reach Garry Point by car drive south on No. 1 Road 5.5 km (3.4 mi) from River Road to Steveston, turn left on Chatham Street and drive 0.7 km (0.4 mi) to the parking area.

Garry Point Park, the Steveston waterfront and Dyke Road along the South Arm of the Fraser River are probably the best spots for gull watching. Look for **Thayer's, Herring, Glaucous-winged, Mew, Ring-billed and Bonaparte's Gulls.**

Having explored the historic Steveston area leave by way of Moncton Road, heading east for 1.6 km (1.0 mi) to No. 2 Road. Turn right, head south for 0.8 km (0.5 mi) to the stop sign, turn left onto Dyke Road and follow this past the fish packing facilities on the right for 0.7 km (0.4 mi) to Gilbert Beach and London Farm. The beach is an area to check for ducks and migrating shorebirds, including **Whimbrel.**

Dyke Road continues along the river for another 1.2 km (0.7 mi) to a parking area at the end of No. 3 Road. This is an area worthy of some walking. Watch for a variety of birds on the river, harbour seals and, in April and May, sea lions. Take the path that heads east. The **Green-backed Heron** can sometimes be found in the slough to the left. **Barn, Tree and Violet-green Swallows** are common throughout the summer. The **Yellow-headed Blackbird** has been seen in the spring and **Northern Shrike** frequent the area in winter. **Savannah Sparrow** can be found here for most of the year; in summer they are abundant and the **Lincoln's Sparrow** can often be found with them in spring and fall.

After about 1.0 km (0.6 mi) the path deviates left to skirt a factory. Follow the path for another 1.0 km (0.6 mi) to the factory gates, cross the road and continue on the path heading back to the river. On the left is an open area of marsh backed by a stand of tall deciduous trees, home for **Sharp-shinned and Cooper's Hawks** from October to April. The railway line from the factory is edged by brambles that play host to many **sparrows** and **finches.** For a longer walk, follow the path along the river until it becomes Dyke Road again. Pass through the small community built on the slough, turn left on No. 4 road, continue to the railway line and head back west along this. **Merlin** is often seen in the area and **American Kestrel** is a summer visitor along with **Common Yellowthroat, Warbling Vireo** and **Mourning Dove**.

From the south end of No. 3 Road drive north for 1.0 km (0.6 mi), turn left on Finn Road, head east for 1.7 km (1.1 mi), turn right onto No. 4 Road and cross Woodward Slough. Check the slough for **ducks. (Hooded Merganser** winter here) and the hedgerows for **sparrows** and **finches.** Continue on No. 4 Road for 0.8 km (0.5 mi), cross the railway line and turn left on Dyke Road. For those venturing out on foot or by bike this point should be reached by taking the path from the parking area at No. 3 Road. Follow Dyke Road along the river, heading east, and check the slough and trees on the right for **Marsh Wren,** raptors and **ducks.** The pumping station at Horseshoe Slough is 1.5 km

(0.9 mi) along Dyke Road. Turn left into the parking area.

Here is the start of a trail that runs north alongside the railway line for 6.5 km (4.0 mi) and provides some of the best habitat for birding on Lulu Island. The southern end runs along Horseshoe Slough through an industrial area but is well protected by stands of tall trees and thick hedgerows. From the industrial area the trail follows Shell Road for about 2.0 km (1.2 mi) until it again becomes a path, now running through Blueberry fields. While the whole trail is worth exploring, the southern end and the northern half provide the best birding. Intermediate points on the trail can be reached by driving 0.2 km (0.1 mi) east on Dyke Road to No. 5 Road, turning left, heading north and turning right on to Steveston Highway, Williams Road, Blundell Road, Granville Avenue or Westminster Highway. Each of these crosses the trail 0.8 km (0.5 mi) west of No. 5 Road.

Hooded Merganser

The hedgerows along this trail provide a year-round home for **Rufous-sided Towhee, Bewick's and Winter Wrens, American Robin, Bushtit, Black-capped Chickadee, House and Purple Finches, Pine Siskin** and **American Goldfinch.** The fall migration brings the **Yellow-rumped Warbler, Western Tanager, Red Crossbill** and birds that winter here such as **Downy Woodpecker, Northern Flicker, Varied Thrush, Dark-eyed Junco, Golden and Ruby-crowned Kinglets** and **White-crowned and Golden-crowned Sparrows.** Spring brings the breeding birds such as **Rufous Hummingbird, Wilson's, Townsend's, Orange-crowned and MacGillivray's Warblers, Black-headed Grosbeak** and **Swainson's Thrush,** while **Hermit Thrush** is a common migrant. Between Francis and Blundell Roads listen for **Willow Flycatcher's** call; each spring these birds return to breed and can be heard on almost any summer day.

Several other areas of Lulu Island are worthy of note. Bridge Point Market at the north end of No. 3 Road provides access to the North and Middle Arms of the Fraser River. There is a small marsh area from which *Common Snipe* are often flushed. Sea Island Bridge leading to the airport provides a viewing platform for the Middle Arm; *Common Merganser* spend the winter months behind the marina to the northeast of the bridge. Watch for *Crested Myna* in this area.

Richmond Nature Park is divided by Highway 99 and No. 5 Road on the north side of Westminster Highway. The western section of the park has trails around the bog. *Wood and Mandarin Ducks* can be found in the winter months. The eastern section of the park is less maintained and gumboots are recommended. *Hutton's Vireo* can be found here in spring and *Great -horned Owl* is a regular visitor.

Triangle Road runs east from the south end of No. 6 Road to the banks of the Fraser River. A trail leads southwest along the river. This is a quiet area where you may see *Black-headed Grosbeak* and *Northern Oriole* during summer. Triangle Road continues north-east along the edge of a landfill site. Look for *Northern Shrike* in autumn and winter.

To the east, Shelter Island Marina at the south end of Graybar Road provides access to paths along Annacis Channel in the South Arm of the Fraser River. Across from the marina are Don and Lion Islands. *Mute Swans* have been breeding here for several years.

The North Fraser River can be viewed from the seawall at the northern end of No. 4 Road, Shell Road or No. 5 Road. From autumn to spring many *gulls* make their home on the log booms along Mitchell Island.

Throughout the area feeders draw a variety of birds and are always worth checking. *Band-tailed Pigeon, Steller's Jay* and *Evening Grosbeak* can be seen and a feeder in the Terra Nova area was the winter home for a *Harris' Sparrow* for several years. Around any open water check for unusual birds such as *Franklin's Gull, Common and Caspian Terns, Semipalmated and Black-bellied Plovers, Dunlin, Sanderling, Western Sandpiper* and *Belted Kingfisher*. Summer skies may reveal a *Common Nighthawk* and in June, *Vaux's and Black Swifts.* Open fields may contain the *Western Meadowlark* in autumn and, in summer, fence posts occasionally provide perching spots for *Eastern and Western Kingbirds.*

BURNABY LAKE REGIONAL PARK
AND DEER LAKE PARK

Burnaby Lake and Deer Lake Parks are two prime birding areas in an urban setting. They offer an escape from the city without leaving the city and provide the opportunity to observe a wide variety of plants, animals, birds, reptiles and invertebrates. They are places to enjoy the passing of the seasons, whether reflected in the seasonally changing bird life, or in the forests, marshes, rivers and fields that make up the area. The two parks, as their names suggest, have as their focal points the lakes that give them their names. Deer Lake is a municipal park, Burnaby Lake a Greater Vancouver Regional District park, and both are located in what is known locally as Burnaby's central valley.

This location provides a pathway for migrating birds through the centre of the city, and as a result, both parks can be exciting places to be in the spring, at the height of migration. The fall migration period tends to be more spread out but, at any season, there is always the chance that the unusual and the occasional rarity will show up. Summer will present the birder with good opportunities to observe many of the typical breeding birds of the forested and freshwater habitats of the Lower Mainland. In winter, the parks are good locations to observe a large variety of the birds that winter in the Lower Mainland or are resident year-round.

The land now occupied by the parks was extensively logged around the turn of the century, and walking the many forest trails, one can see much evidence of this activity. Large western red cedar stumps with the springboard holes still visible are found throughout. The remnants of a sawmill can be identified just west of the Nature House at Burnaby Lake from the large mound of sawdust and wood waste now being colonized by birch trees.

The two parks occupy an area dominated by lowland, second growth, mixed forest habitat which, in both cases, forms the larger part of the lands surrounding the lakes. Burnaby Lake has fairly extensive marshes surrounding most of its shoreline and these reach their greatest extent at its eastern end where the outlet to the lake becomes the Brunette River that flows to the Fraser River. Feeding Burnaby Lake from the east is Still Creek, and from the south, flowing in to the lake, is the outlet stream from Deer Lake Creek. So, both parks belong to a common watershed, but where Still Creek and many of the other lesser streams that feed Burnaby Lake flow through industrial as well as residential areas, the many small streams that feed Deer Lake flow out of forested and/or residential areas with almost no industry. Although both lakes suffer from pollution and an excess of nutrients flowing into them from residential neighbour-hoods, Deer Lake is generally suffering less than Burnaby Lake.

While Burnaby Lake has extensive marshland, Deer Lake has very little. But what it lacks in marshland it makes up for in the fairly extensive area of rough grassland at its western end. Close to the shore at the lake's northwest corner is a small remnant sphagnum bog. This modest but interesting variety of forests, marshland, bogs, rough meadow/grassland and freshwater streams and lakes along with the gardens and mowed playing fields is the basis for the variety of birds and other wildlife that occupy the parks and is so much a part of their attraction.

DIRECTIONS

Burnaby Lake Regional Park

The Trans Canada Highway (Highway 1) is the easiest access route to both parks. To get to the Nature House on Burnaby Lake, a good starting place for a birding walk, take the Kensington North exit from Highway 1 and drive about 2 km (1.2 mi) north. Follow the signs for Lougheed Highway east and as you come down the offramp after passing over Still Creek on the Kensington overpass, turn right immediately on to Winston Street. Follow this road east to Piper Avenue. Turn right, following the sign to Burnaby Lake Regional Park. Park at the south end of Piper Avenue after crossing the railway tracks.

Alternatively, the Cariboo North exit from Highway 1 can be taken. Follow Cariboo Road north under Gaglardi Way until it intersects with Winston Street. Turn left and follow Winston Street west to Piper Avenue. Turn left onto Piper Avenue into the park.

Another suitable place for parking at Burnaby Lake is at the foot of Avalon Avenue which is a left turn off Cariboo Road about 0.5 km (0.3 mi) south of its intersection with Winston Street. Also, one can park at the Burnaby Lake Sports complex. Head north on Kensington Avenue after exiting Highway 1 and turn right on to Sprott Street or, continue south on Sperling Avenue off Sprott Street and find parking in the Rowing Club parking lot at the end of Roberts Street.

Deer Lake Park

Take the Willingdon South exit off Highway 1. Turn left at the first set of traffic lights on to Canada Way east and follow it to Royal Oak Avenue. Turn right on to Royal Oak Avenue and drive south through the four-way stop at the Moscrop/Gilpin intersection. The entrance to the park and the small parking lot is on the left approximately 0.5 km (0.3 mi) south of the four-way stop.

Other points of access to Deer Lake Park are from the parking area around the James

Cowan Theatre and the Burnaby Art Gallery. To get here take the Kensington South exit off Highway 1 and follow it to Canada Way. Turn right (west) on Canada Way and then take the first left on to Deer Lake Drive and then left on to Gilpin Avenue. The parking lot entrances are on the right at the top of the hill. To access the east end of Deer Lake at the public beach, follow the signs to Deer Lake Beach on Highway 1. These signs will take you via Kensington and Canada Way to Burris Street and then to Buckingham Avenue. Follow Buckingham Avenue west to the parking area just left of the intersection of Buckingham and Sperling Avenues.

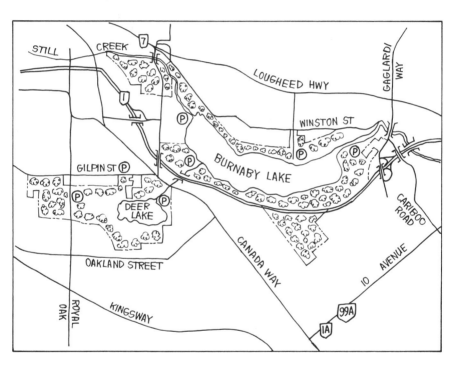

Burnaby Lake and Deer Lake

BIRD SPECIES

The birdlife of both parks is similar, particularly the birds that make use of the forest and freshwater habitats. One could expect to see most species discussed here in either park. To avoid much unnecessary repetition, an emphasis on winter species is found in the Burnaby Lake description and spring species in the Deer Lake description. This is not a recommendation to visit these areas in these seasons only.

Burnaby Lake Regional Park

Starting at the Nature House parking area at Burnaby Lake, one can pick up the trail that heads east and is signposted to the Cariboo Dam. Walking this trail takes one through an attractive sample of the mixed forest that is very typical of the area and contains the birds one would expect to see in this habitat. In the forest, look for ***Black-capped and Chestnut-backed Chickadees*** often, in the cooler months, found in mixed flocks with ***Golden-crowned and Ruby-crowned Kinglets, Red-breasted Nuthatch,*** and the occasional ***Brown Creeper***. Also look for ***Downy Woodpecker***, and the less common ***Hairy Woodpecker***. In the understory, ***Winter Wren, Bewick's Wren, Song Sparrow, Dark-eyed Junco*** and ***Rufous-sided Towhee*** are common. At all times the raucous ***Steller's Jay*** is a noisy presence in the forest as is the ***Northwestern Crow*** and less frequently, ***Common Raven***. In fall, winter, and early spring these forested areas often have flocks of ***Pine Siskin, Evening Grosbeak*** and ***Red Crossbill*** feeding in the upper stories of the forest.

One can continue to walk along this trail, cross the Brunette River and circumnavigate the lake. However, we will return to our starting point just south of the Nature House. Heading south, the pathway extends out into the lake on a raised promontory with a beaver lodge at its far end. This location provides excellent viewing up and down the lake and over the surrounding marshes where, in spring and summer, ***Red-winged Blackbird*** and ***Marsh Wren*** are common. ***Northern Harrier*** and less commonly ***Short-eared Owl*** both hunt over these marshes. The large black cottonwood trees that

American and Eurasian Wigeon

border the lake often provide perches for ***Bald Eagle*** in fall and winter as do the large wooden pylons in the lake which are also used by ***Double-crested Cormorant.*** Immediately in front of you in this location is an area of mudflats where ***Long-billed Dowitcher, Dunlin, Greater Yellowlegs*** and ***Pectoral Sandpiper*** can be seen in migration along with the resident ***Great Blue Heron***. From this location and others around the lake, ***American Bittern*** can be heard booming in the spring. In the fall look for ***Green-backed Heron*** and in winter, ***Northern Shrike***. ***Virginia Rail*** are resident in the marshes year-round except when the area freezes hard. The lake itself offers many species of duck throughout the seasons: ***Green-winged Teal, Mallard, Northern Pintail, Northern Shoveler, Gadwall, American Widgeon, Canvasback, Greater and Lesser Scaup, Common Goldeneye, Bufflehead, Common Merganser***, the occasional ***Blue-winged Teal*** in summer and even on one Christmas count, ***Cinnamon Teal.*** In and around the stream flowing into the lake south of the Nature House are large numbers of resident ***Wood Duck.***

There are many points of access to the lake and its environs and exploration on foot is recommended. In all seasons the chance of the interesting and the unusual is possible. Such birds as ***Red-throated Pipit, Black-and-white Warbler, Tennesee Warbler, Yellow-headed Blackbird, Eastern Kingbird, Lapland Longspur, Ross' Goose*** and on the playing fields at the west end of the lake, ***Buff -breasted Sandpiper***, have all been recorded. More common species include ***Red-eyed Vireo*** and ***Western Wood-Pewee.***

Deer Lake Park

The walk in to Deer Lake Park from the parking lot at the foot of the hill on Royal Oak Avenue is an excellent place to look for spring migrants in the forest, hedges and, meadows. April and May should produce ***warblers: Orange-crowned, Yellow-rumped, Black-throated Gray, Townsend's, MacGillivray's, Yellow and Wilson's.*** The ***Warbling Vireo*** is a common migrant and ***Hutton's Vireo*** an uncommon resident. To the south, the path takes one out into the rough grass meadows, where ***Ring-necked Pheasant*** is common. This is a good location to see breeding ***Common Yellowthroat*** and ***Savannah Sparrow*** and, in spring, ***Golden-crowned and White-crowned Sparrows*** in migration. Flocks of ***Bushtit*** are regular in the cooler months and the ***American Goldfinch*** is seen all year. In fall, winter and spring, ***Lincoln's Sparrow and Fox Sparrow*** are found around the meadows, the latter particularly where there are extensive blackberry thickets.

A walk around this meadow area may also be very productive for seeing raptors. The ***Red-tailed Hawk*** nests in the park and occasionally ***Rough-legged Hawk*** is found in winter. ***Merlin*** and ***American Kestrel*** are regular but uncommon and rarely ***Peregrine Falcon*** is seen in fall and winter. ***Cooper's and Sharp-shinned Hawks*** are regular in fall and winter. Following the path that skirts the meadows to the south and heading east, one can walk toward the forest that flanks the southeast slope of the park. In spring and summer one can expect a wide variety of species including **Black-headed Grosbeak, Brown-headed Cowbird, Brewer's Blackbird, Willow Flycatcher** and less commonly **Olive-sided Flycatcher, Pacific-slope Flycatcher** and in migration **Hammond's Flycatcher. Northern Flicker** numbers often swell considerably in the fall. Unusual spring migrants seen in the meadow area include **Western Kingbird** and **Mountain Bluebird.**

There are many trails that can be taken into the forested areas from the meadows. A suggested route is to follow the meadow trail to its eastern terminus at the chain-link fence that used to be the old boundary to the park. Walk into the forest at this point and follow an informal trail east and uphill through the forest. This area is the most reliable for **Pileated Woodpecker,** and in winter, may also produce **Red-breasted Sapsucker. Swainson's Thrush** are common in summer as are **Varied Thrush** in the winter when the occasional **Hermit Thrush** may be seen too. **Owls** are not numerous in the park but this forested area has produced a number of species, most commonly **Western Screech, Northern Saw-whet, and Barred.** At other locations in the park, **Great Horned, Long-eared and Barn Owls** have also been seen. This latter species may now be absent from the park following the destruction of the old buildings in which it nested that were part of the Oakalla Prison complex.

Following this path through the forest, one eventually emerges from the park at its extreme southeast corner and into a residential area on Strawson Avenue. The forest at this point is a regular place to see **Band-tailed Pigeon** perched in the tops of the tall western hemlock. Continuing east on to Haszard will bring one to the steps that lead once again down to the lake, this time to the beach area at its eastern end. The lake may now be followed around its northern shore. **Belted Kingfisher** can be seen around the lake; in winter. **Hooded Merganser** is numerous and one can expect to see **Ruddy Duck** and more rarely **Ring-necked Duck.** Joining the resident flocks of **Canada Goose** is the occasional **Greater White-fronted Goose.** In spring the lake is a good location to watch *swallows* in migration, some of which remain all summer. **Tree, Violet-green and Barn Swallows** are the most common and more unusually, **Northern Rough-winged and Cliff Swallows.** A few *gulls* also use the lake and beach area with the **Ring-billed Gull** commonly resident in winter. The occasional **Glaucous-winged and Thayer's Gulls** also put in an appearance. The lake also attracts a number of other interesting but transient species including, in the late summer months, **Caspian Tern** and *Osprey* and, in spring, the occasional **Common Loon** on the lake.

Both parks offer a remarkable variety of birds, given their location in such a residential area, and can repay the birdwatcher handsomely for time spent in walking their trails and paths throughout the seasons.

Tucked beneath the shadow of Burke Mountain in northeast Coquitlam, less than an hour from Vancouver, lie Minnekhada Regional Park and Addington Marsh. Contiguous with each other, they provide over 450 ha (1,110 ac) of very productive birding. The area is bordered by Burke Mountain to the west, undeveloped crown lands on the north, the Pitt River to the east, and to the south by abandoned farmland and the Pitt River Dike-DeBouville Slough trail system.

Once a private hunting preserve, the 175 ha Minnekhada (meaning "Rattling Waters") farm became a regional park in 1984. The previous owners, two former Lieutenant-Governors, keen hunters both, created a large wetland in the centre of the park to attract waterfowl. Today, this is still a productive waterfowl spot, particularly in winter. The elegant Minnekhada Lodge is open to visitors every Sunday from 1:00-4:00 p.m. April through October, and every first and third Sunday the rest of the year except in January when it is closed.

The adjacent Addington Marsh, also once a private hunting preserve of approximately 283 ha (700 ac), was purchased in 1977 by the Nature Trust of B.C. in order to create a wildlife reserve. Today it is managed by Ducks Unlimited and the Ministry of Environment, Lands and Parks.

Minnekhada Park lies within the Coastal Western Hemlock Zone. Together with Addington Marsh the area offers exceptionally varied terrain. Coniferous forest, mixed and deciduous woods, rocky outcrops, forested slopes, open fields, marshes, sloughs, riverine habitat and riparian vegetation combine to provide excellent birding opportunities in a relatively small area.

DIRECTIONS

To reach Minnekhada Regional Park from Vancouver take the Lougheed Highway (Highway 7) east. At the intersection with the Barnet Highway in Coquitlam turn right (east) staying on the Lougheed, and continue for 3.5 km (2.2 mi) to Coast Meridian Road. Turn left (north) onto Coast Meridian Road. Drive 2.5 km (1.5 mi) to Apel Drive, turn right, and right again after 0.7 km (0.4 mi) onto Victoria Drive. Continue for 1 km (0.6 mi) and turn left staying on Victoria Drive. At the junction with Gilley's Trail, Victoria Drive becomes Quarry Road. Continue on Quarry Road and turn right into the Quarry Road parking lot for the park trailhead.

To get to Minnekhada Lodge follow the same route but turn right onto Gilley's Trail and drive 0.5 km (0.3 mi) to a T-junction. Turn left onto Oliver Road and continue down the single lane road for 1.2 km (0.7 mi) turning left onto the park road. Parking is behind the Lodge. Note: the Lodge is frequently rented for private functions, particularly on summer weekends and access may be restricted or denied to this parking lot during these times. Pit toilets are available at both parking lots, and picnic tables near the Lodge. Park brochures can be picked up at either location.

Addington Marsh can be accessed via the park trail system or from Oliver Road.

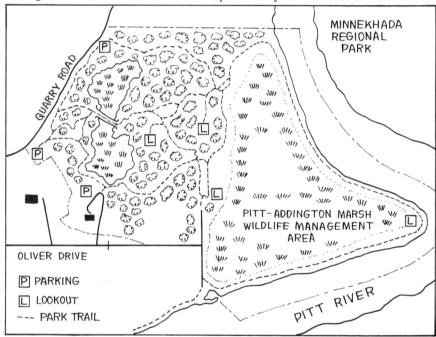

Minnekhada Regional Park and Addington Marsh

BIRD SPECIES

Minnekhada Regional Park

Minnekhada Regional Park has superb scenery, good woodland and marsh walks, and provides interesting birding in varied habitat on a year-round basis. It provides the opportunity to see good numbers of all the common birds of woodland, marsh and field as well as the chance to find some unusual birds. Some of the rarer species that have turned up over the years include a ***Poorwill*** and ***White-throated and Chipping Sparrows***. The combined bird list for Minnekhada and Addington now stands at 145 species.

The marsh in the centre of Minnekhada Park provides one of the more interesting birding spots. To reach it follow the trail from the Quarry Road parking lot and turn left at the first fork. At the second fork take the right trail, and at the third fork the left trail. A few metres after the last fork a rocky outcrop allows you to scan the marsh.

Continue down the trail to the dike (which divides the Upper from the Lower Marsh) and scan the Upper marsh from the dike. At least 19 species of waterfowl have been counted from this point. Winter is the best time for waterfowl watching when good numbers of **Ring-necked Duck** can be seen, as well as **Lesser Scaup, American**

American Coot

Wigeon, Green-winged Teal, Common Goldeneye and Common and Hooded Merganser. In spring look for *Cinnamon and Blue-winged Teal* and *Wood Duck,* as well as more common duck species. *Ruddy Duck* has turned up at least once. *Great Blue Heron* can be found all year. They nest in good numbers at the nearby DeBouville Slough. Watch for the occasional beaver and river otter. Five species of *swallow* can be observed from the dike. The Lower Marsh is thickly vegetated with spirea and holds large numbers of the *Marsh Wren* all year and *Common Yellowthroat* in summer. *Sora, Virginia Rail , Pied-billed Grebe* and *American Coot* may also be found.

In forests look for *Hairy, Downy and Pileated Woodpeckers, Steller's Jay,* both *Black-capped and Chestnut-backed Chickadees, Red-breasted Nuthatch, Brown Creeper, Golden-crowned Kinglet, Winter Wren, Rufous-sided Towhee, Evening Grosbeak, Red Crossbill* and *Pine Siskin* at any time of year. The *Great Horned Owl* inhabits the park, and one of the best places to see it is on the south side, along the Panabode Trail near the marsh, just east of the picnic area. Listen for *Western Screech-Owl* and *Northern Saw-whet Owl* anywhere in the park. *Common Raven* is resident and may be seen or heard anywhere in the area. The *Northern Flicker* tends to be more common in the park in fall and winter. Watch for *Varied Thrush* and *Dark-eyed Junco* in winter.

Check out the Low Knoll (reached from the Dike Trail) where *Northern Pygmy Owl* has been found. There are splendid views from this knoll across the south marsh, the Pitt River and beyond. Scan the marsh for *Northern Harrier*, and look for *Black and Vaux's Swifts, Red-tailed Hawk* and other raptors soaring above.

Ruffed Grouse is a species becoming increasingly difficult to find around Vancouver. It may occur anywhere in the park but especially on the North Trail, and near Oliver Road. *Blue Grouse* are heard more often than seen, particularly in spring. You may see black bear, black-tailed deer, and coyote if you are lucky.

Summer brings *Swainson's Thrush, Western Tanager, Hammond's and Pacific-slope Flycatchers. Hermit Thrush* nests on the slopes of Burke Mountain and can be found passing through the park on migration. Mixed flocks of *warblers* feed their way through the park in fall, particularly on the edges between the coniferous and deciduous woods. Look for *Orange-crowned, Yellow-rumped, Black-throated Gray, Townsend's, and Wilson's Warblers* in large flocks.

Deciduous woods, mostly of red alder, form a small part of the park. The dense understorey of salmonberry provides protected nesting for *Bewick's Wren, Rufous-sided Towhee,* and *Song Sparrow.* Watch for *Rufous Hummingbird, Western Wood-Pewee, Red-eyed and Warbling Vireos, Orange-crowned and Black-throated Gray Warblers*, and *Black-headed Grosbeak* in summer.

From the Panabode Trail a side trail leads to the Addington Marsh Lookout with excellent views over the marsh (see section on the marsh below). A short path leads from the Lookout to the road below. Addington Marsh is now on the left; to the right the woods hold nesting *Red-breasted Sapsucker* and *Hairy Woodpecker*. Oliver Road runs west (or right) a few hundred metres on. To the left some excellent old field habitat (not part of the park) sometimes has *Short-eared Owl* and usually has *Northern Shrike* in winter. The hedgerows and thickets lining the road host a variety of *sparrow* species, including *Fox, Lincoln's, Golden-crowned and White-crowned Sparrows* in fall and winter. In spring and summer watch for *Willow Flycatcher, Yellow and MacGillivray's*

Warblers and *Common Yellowthroat*. *Bushtit* nest in good numbers by the roadside, constructing their nests in the young alder and spirea. *Gray Catbird* has occasionally been found along this stretch in summer. Also in summer look for *Band-tailed Pigeon* which descends from its nesting area on Burke Mountain to feed on berries and fruits.

Continue west on Oliver Road and take the first right towards Minnekhada Lodge. *Eastern and Western Kingbirds* in summer, and *Northern Shrike* in winter have all been found in the fields on either side of the Lodge Road. Early spring floods turn these and adjacent fields into instant ponds attacting scores of ducks which can be easily observed from the road. Other species such as *Greater and Lesser Yellowlegs, Great Blue Heron* and *American Bittern* also use these flooded areas. To get back to the Quarry Road parking lot (a 20 minute walk) go left past the picnic tables, skirting the marsh. When the trail emerges into the open scan the High Knoll where *Turkey Vulture* is sometimes observed soaring along the edge.

Addington Marsh

Addington Marsh is best surveyed from the vantage point of the Lookout. A spotting scope makes viewing easier and is essential for the further reaches of the marsh. In spring it is possible to record 50 species or more in one hour from this spot. Look for *Pied-billed Grebe, Green-backed Heron* (which nests along DeBouville Slough), *Sandhill Crane, American Bittern, Peregrine Falcon, California Gull,* and *American Pipit,* to name only a few. The early spring eulachon run attracts thousands of *Mew Gulls* to the Pitt River by Addington. In summer a good concentation of *Osprey* nest on the pilings lining the river. Look for *Rough-legged Hawk, Bald Eagle, Trumpeter Swan* and the occasional *Tundra Swan* and *Thayer's Gull* in winter.

Access to the trail around Addington Marsh can be gained from the Lookout above the marsh (head north on the trail), from the Minnekhada Loop Trail, or from the southern end of the marsh near the caretaker's cottage (south of the end of Oliver Road). The trail to the marsh is not signed or marked once it leaves Minnekhada Park, although where it skirts the marsh it runs on top of the dike making it impossible to get lost. The trail can be quite overgrown with blackberries at times making walking difficult. Two towers enroute offer good views across both river and marsh.

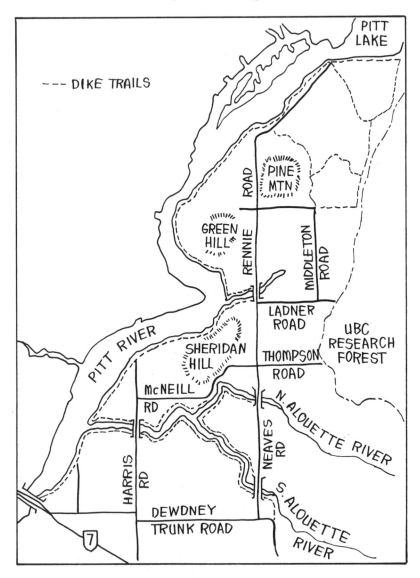

Pitt Wildlife Management Area

PITT WILDLIFE MANAGEMENT AREA AND VICINITY

Pitt Meadows is 40 km (25 mi) east of Vancouver North of the Fraser River. It is a narrow valley 12 km (7.5 mi) long bordered by the Pitt River and the Coast Mountains. Pitt Lake immediately north is 26 km (16.1 mi) long. The lake drains an area as far north as Mt. Garibaldi on the Squamish-Whistler highway.

The Pitt River was named by James McMillan in 1827, possibly to honour William Pitt (The Elder), Earl of Chatham and twice Prime Minister of England. In the early 1870's the first white settlers in the area diked portions of the Alouette and Pitt Rivers. The disastrous flooding of 1894 was followed by a more complete diking programme. The northern part of the valley (north of Sturgeon Slough) was marshland until the early 1950's when the Dutch under the guidance of Dr. Blom began a programme of diking and ditching to reclaim the 2,900 ha (7,160 ac) we now know as Pitt Polder. This had been attempted previously in 1911 and again in the 1920s when a Mennonite settlement there was flooded.

From Highway 7 (Lougheed Highway) north to just past Sturgeon Slough, much of the land is dairy pasture together with some production of soft fruits, blueberry, raspberry, and commercial horticultural enterprises. Passing under the hydro powerline however, the ground becomes wetter and the marsh predominates, with hardhack, cattail and sedge. Because of the dikes, pumphouses and controlled floodgates into the Pitt River, these are now freshwater marshes. Historically they must have been brackish as both the Pitt and Fraser Rivers are tidal. There are a few thickets of willow and alder which provide good cover for birds.

There are three hills on the floodplain. Menzies Mountain, now called Sheridan Hill, is the highest at about 100 m (330 ft). It lies along the edge of the Pitt River between the North Alouette River and Sturgeon Slough. Green Hill is 2 km (1.2 mi) to the north, and Pine Mountain 1 km (0.6 mi) further north and to the east of Rennie Road. This last is in the Pitt Bog Ecological Reserve. All three hills are well treed, Sheridan and Green with Douglas fir, western red cedar, vine maple, alder, willow, and birch. Pine Mountain was burned over twice by the Dutch in the early 1950s and has a narrow band of lodgepole and white pine as well as most of the other species already mentioned. Sheridan Hill is private land dotted with homes, Green is in the centre of a private Golf and Country Club, and Pine Mountain is an Ecological Reserve.

DIRECTIONS

There are no gas stations, stores, restaurants or washrooms in the valley (except two outhouses at Pitt Lake);for any of these services return to Highway 7 (Lougheed Highway) and the communities of Pitt Meadows or Maple Ridge.

To reach Pitt Meadows take Highway 1 (Trans Canada Highway) East to Exit 44, marked "Highway 7/Port Coquitlam/Maple Ridge" and after leaving the freeway take the right hand fork to United Blvd. In 0.6 km (0.4 mi) turn sharp left to United Boulevard North and a traffic light. Proceed through this light and you are on the Mary Hill bypass with Colony Farm on your left (another good birding area) and the Fraser River on the right. The bypass ends in 7.4 km (4.6 mi) at the junction with Highway 7. Turn right and in 0.5 km (0.3 mi) cross the Pitt River, then left in 0.6 km (0.4 mi) at a traffic light onto the Dewdney Trunk Road. This is the southern edge of the area described.

A second route is to take the Lougheed Highway through Burnaby and Port Coquitlam to the Pitt River bridge. A third route is to take East Hastings Street in Vancouver, through Burnaby to the Barnett Highway, then along the edge of Burrard Inlet to Port Moody. Here one once again picks up the Lougheed Highway and the Pitt River bridge.

BIRD SPECIES

Travel East on the Dewdney Trunk Road for 2.3 km (1.4 mi) to a T-junction with Harris Road and turn left. Harris Road is not named at the junction. The fields along both roads are good for raptors during the winter months and in migration - *Red-tailed and Rough-legged Hawks, Bald and* occasionally *Golden Eagles, Cooper's and Sharp-shinned Hawks, Northern Harrier and Northern Shrike.* The hedgerows will hold *White-crowned and Golden-crowned Sparrows, Fox Sparrow* and *Western Meadowlark.* In summer months this is a good area for *American Kestrel.*

Continue north on Harris Road, cross the Alouette River in 2.4 km (1.5 mi), looking for waterfowl in the winter months, and in a further 0.7 km (0.4 mi) turn right onto McNeill Road. To your left the area we are heading for starts to open up, ringed on the eastern side of the valley by the mountains of Golden Ears Provincial Park - Alouette, Blanshard (which forms the 'Ears' of the Park), Howay, and Robie Reid. The low rounded peaks to west of Pitt Lake are un-named on most maps. Behind and to the left are Widgeon Peak and Coquitlam Mountain, and, further back, Peneplain and Obelisk Mountains.

McNeil Road skirts around the base of Sheridan Hill while the dike on your right encloses the North Alouette River. The mixed woodland at the base of the hill is home to a rich assortment of birds at most seasons. In summer, *Rufous Hummingbird, Western and Willow Flycatchers, Red-eyed and Warbling Vireos, Cedar Waxwing, Swainson's Thrush, and Orange-crowned, Wilson's and Yellow Warblers.* The adjoining area also supports the Lower Mainland's largest concentration of *Osprey* which nest on the many wooden pilings lining the Pitt River immediately west. In 3.8 km (2.4 mi) McNeil meets Neaves/Rennie Road, the main north/south artery in Pitt

Meadows. The names change at McNeil Road, Neaves Road leading off to the south on your right, Rennie Road to your left.

A short side trip can be taken here by crossing over Neaves/Rennie and travelling Thompson Road (the No Through Road) opposite which ends at a gravel road in 1.4 km (0.9 mi). Park and walk the gravel up the hill. Listen for *warblers* and *vireos* in spring and summer. Check the brushy fields for *sparrows* and *Common Snipe* in the winter months. The slough attracts *Belted Kingfisher* at all seasons. Retrace your route to Neaves/Rennie turn right and head north into the mountains.

In 1.8 km (1.1 mi) from the turning a wooden bridge crosses Sturgeon Slough. Park immediately after the bridge. Walk the gravel road on the north side of the slough for 0.75 km (0.5 mi) to the junction with the Pitt River dike. The brush at the western end of Sturgeon Slough occasionally holds *Green-backed Heron.* The trees on the Pitt River attract *warblers* and *vireos* in spring and summer. The weedy field to the north may contain both *Mountain and Western Bluebirds* in spring migration, lots of *Savannah Sparrow*, and an occasional

Eastern Kingbird

Lincoln's Sparrow. *Willow Flycatcher* may sometimes be seen in the Alder. In the winter the slough has *Common Goldeneye, Bufflehead, Horned Grebe* and *Belted Kingfisher.*

Continue north along Rennie Road. After 2 km (1.2 mi) a powerline crosses the valley. The field on both sides of the road should be carefully checked for *Sandhill Crane,* which can be found at any season. Prior to the powerline being constructed they were more common. The fields on the east side may contain *Bald and Golden Eagles,* and in the summer months, *Turkey Vulture.* *Bald Eagle* is a permanent resident of the valley while *Golden Eagle* is rare (although there are nesting records in Pitt Meadows for this species).

About 300 m (990 ft) north of the powerline a gravel road leads off to both left and right. The left (western) side is gated and locked and leads in 2.1 km (1.3 mi) to the Pitt River dike. The habitat is cottonwood/alder/birch and the hike a pleasant one but there is unlikely to be anything along this trail that cannot be found elsewhere in the Pitt. The gravel road to the east is rough and potholed. In 1.7 km (1.1 mi) it turns to the south. Park here and check out the various sloughs beyond the yellow gate. In summer both **Eastern and Western Kingbirds** can be found, while over Homilkum Marsh to the northeast you may see **Sandhill Crane, Pied-billed Grebe, Cinnamon and Blue-winged Teal,** and **Black and Vaux's Swifts**. These last two species nest in the steep cliffs and the trees of the U.B.C. Research Forest which forms the eastern edge of the valley. Check the power pylons for raptors but ignore the plastic **Great Horned Owl** perched atop the pylon nearest the corner!

Drive southwards along the gravel road (paved after 1 km (0.6 mi) and now named Middleton Road), turn right in 2.4 km (1.5 mi) onto Ladner Road then right again in 1.7 km back onto Rennie Road. The gravel road you started down is 2.4 km (1.5 mi) to the north. This route may be closing off in the future making Ladner/Middleton Roads the only access to Homilkum Marsh and the Ecological Reserve of Pine Mountain.

Travelling further north on Rennie Road we run into a band of dark coniferous trees on both sides of the road. To the east is the Ecological Reserve on the slopes of Pine Mountain (presently off limits to birders and botanists but there are plans to open up an access from the southeast corner). On a walk along Rennie Road through this band of trees you could see **Black-headed Grosbeak, Willow and Western Flycatchers, Orange-crowned and Yellow Warblers, Cedar Waxwing, Black-capped and Chest-nut-backed Chickadees, Red-breasted Nuthatch** and **Brown Creeper.**

In a further 1.5 km (0.9 mi) north, Rennie Road bisects the Pitt River dike and bends to the right. From here to the stand of tall cottonwood trees 1.2 km (0.7 mi) further along, the roadside habitat to the west should be carefully checked in summer for **Gray Catbird.** This is the most reliable spot in the Lower Mainland to find the **catbird** which frequently sings in the early morning and later on overcast days. The cottonwood stand also holds **Western Tanager, Downy Woodpecker** and **Red-breasted Nuthatch**. The open fields on the eastern side again should be looked over for **Sandhill Crane** and **Osprey. Northern Harrier** and **Short-eared Owl** are also attracted to this area in winter months.

Rennie Road ends at Pitt Lake in a further 2 km (1.2 mi). There is a boat launch and some rough parking for cars. This area becomes very congested on summer weekends and a certain amount of vehicle vandalism occurs so be careful to lock your car securely and hide valuable possessions.

A system of trails and dikes lead off from here that make this the most productive birding spot in the entire Pitt Meadows area (see map). Late spring and summer bring in a number of species that are rarely found elsewhere in the Lower Mainland of

Vancouver. There is a dike walk around the triangular Katsie Marsh, with two observation towers giving views out over the marsh. The area is productive at any season. It is about a one and a half hour walk to the first tower. All of the woodland species previously mentioned (with perhaps the exception of *Gray Catbird*) can be found along the Nature Dike. Look for *Black-throated Gray Warbler, Townsend's Warbler, Red-breasted Sapsucker, Hairy Woodpecker, Northern Oriole, and Marsh and Bewick's Wrens.* Rarities along this trail have been *Least Flycatcher, Nashville Warbler* and *American Redstart*. Listen and look for *Common Snipe* winnowing over the marsh. The many nesting boxes along this trail are used by *Wood Duck* and *Hooded Merganser.*

In winter months the other two arms of the marsh, Pitt Lake Dike and Swan Dike will prove equally productive with a wide assortment of waterfowl. *American and Eurasian Wigeon, Northern Pintail, Gadwall, Green-winged Teal, scaup, goldeneye, Western and Horned Grebes,* and *Common and Hooded Mergansers.* There are usually many *Swans* here too, both *Tundra and Trumpeter,* and in hard winters further north, *Snow Bunting* and *Common Redpoll* have been found along the dikes. The entire walk of the Katsie Marsh perimeter will take 2 - 2 1/2 hours, longer if the birding is good, and will usually produce something out of the ordinary.

Both Pitt River and Lake are frequented by a small gull assortment, mostly in the winter months. Look for *Glaucous-winged, Mew, Ring-billed, Herring and Thayer's gulls.* In warmer months you may find *Bonaparte's Gull* and maybe a *Caspian or Common Tern*, the latter in migration.

One cannot give an account of Pitt Meadows without mentioning the dike walks, indeed this is what likely attracts the non-birder to the area. There are over 50 km (31 mi) of readily accessible dikes which can be walked or cycled and we urge you to get a map and explore these. The 1:50,000 series maps put out by Energy Mines and Resources Canada are ideal for this purpose; the Port Coquitlam sheet covers 95% of the area discussed here.

The dike from Highway 7, south down the Pitt River and around the corner to the Fraser River, then east to the Pitt Meadows Airport, provides probably the best potential habitat in the Lower Mainland for *bluebirds* in migration. There are cultivated fields, still with real hedgerows around them, and on the riverside, huge stands of cottonwood/alder with brushy thickets at their bases. This section is only 6 km (3.7 mi) long and road accessible from both ends.

Another walk is from the Harris Road bridge over the Alouette River, west down the Alouette to the Pitt River, then northeast to Sheridan Hill, 5 km (3.1 mi) one way, walk back birding Harris Road. On a bicycle this route takes one hour. There are five *Osprey* nests on the pilings in the river along this section of the dike.

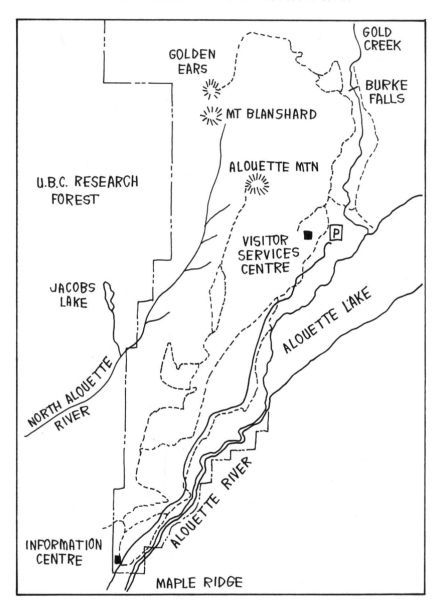

Golden Ears Provincial Park

GOLDEN EARS PROVINCIAL PARK

Golden Ears Provincial Park lies in the Coast Mountains about 48 km east of Vancouver on the north side of the Fraser River. From its southern boundary near Maple Ridge, the park extends 55 km northward through mountain wilderness to the southern boundary of Garibaldi Provincial Park.

Lowland forests are second growth with significant old growth at higher elevations and remote valleys. The park encompasses three Biogeoclimatic Zones: (1) The Coastal Hemlock Zone (at elevations up to 1,000 m (3,300 ft) depending on slope); (2) The Mountain Hemlock Zone (at elevations above 1,000 m (3,300 ft)); (3) The Alpine Tundra Zone (elevations above the timberline + 1,500 m (4,950 ft) approximately).

The park contains a number of quite distinct aquatic habitats including: (1) Alouette Lake - 2.5 km (1.5 mi) long, a fjord-like lake which is deep and cold (actually a B.C. Hydro reservoir) with little shore vegetation. The lake supports fish populations and is thus attractive to birds such as *mergansers*, (2) Mike Lake - a small shallow lake surrounded by bog vegetation with well developed emergent shore vegetation, and floating species. Mike Lake is the richest bird area in the park, which is no doubt a reflection of the different vegetation community interfaces creating good "edge effect".

In addition to the "natural" habitats, there are several human modified areas including the two campgrounds and the large day-use area with its vast expanse of lawns.

DIRECTIONS

From Vancouver - the park is located 48 km (30 mi) east of Vancouver, near Maple Ridge. From Highway 1, look for the Maple Ridge exit just before the Port Mann Bridge. Follow the Mary Hill Bypass to the Lougheed Highway. Turn right and cross the Pitt River Bridge and continue to Maple Ridge. Watch for signs in town directing you to the park. If following 232nd Street, go north to Fern Crescent (the road that leads to the park). Once you are in downtown Maple Ridge (Haney), the route is well-signed. The route is also signed from the east. Total travel time from Vancouver is about 1 hour. A 10 km (6.2 mi) paved highway extends from the park entrance to the day-use areas campgrounds and Gold Creek corridor.

A park brochure containing a map is available. The park has an extensive trail system but for naturalists four are recommended:

(1)   Mike Lake Trail - 4.2 km (2.6 mi) from park entrance to Mike Lake. Trail round lake is about 3 km (1.9 mi). It takes 2-3 hours and has an elevation change of 100 m (330 ft). You can also drive right to the lake.

(2)   Alouette Mountain Hiking Trail - top of Incline Trail via Lake Beautiful to Alouette Mountain, 10 km (6.2 mi) and takes about 5 hours. This is the best access to the Mountain Hemlock Zone forest and sub-alpine habitats.

(3)   Gold Creek Corridor - West Canyon Parking Lot to Lake Viewpoint is 3 km (1.9 mi) long and takes about 2 hours with an elevation change of 150 m (495 ft)

(4)   West Canyon to Alder Flats is 5 km (3.1 mi) and takes about 3 hours with minimal elevation change. The Gold Creek Corridor is a scenic area with good birding and an opportunity to view Mountain goats (Evans Peak).

Please remember that the Park's back country is extremely rugged and hiking in this area should be attempted only by experienced and properly equipped mountaineers.

BIRD SPECIES

Some 141 species have been recorded in Golden Ears Provincial Park. Bird study began in the park in 1962 at which time an annotated checklist of the Southern Portion (now Golden Ears) of Garibaldi Provincial Park was prepared. A more extensive report by Al Grass was published in 1989.

Blue Grouse are seen at all elevations but the best area is along the Alouette Mountain or West Canyon trails. They are often heard "hooting", in spring. *Barred Owl* is a resident and is best seen at Mike Lake, Alouette Campground (Tiarella Nature Trail). Both *Black and Vaux's Swifts* are summer residents. They are often seen on low cloudy days, especially by Gold Creek Corridor (Lower Falls Trail).

Six species of *woodpeckers* occur here, including the *Red-breasted Sapsucker* . Look for its wells on western hemlock bark by Mike Lake, Spirea Nature Trail, Alouette Campground. The *Warbling Vireo* is quite abundant here, especially around Mike Lake.

There is a good *warbler* migration in spring including *Wilson's, MacGillivray's, and Yellow-rumped* (both *Audubon's and Myrtle* type). The *Black-throated Gray and Townsend's Warblers* are summer residents.

Both *Red and White-winged Crossbills* are found here (highly cyclic in abundance but often in good numbers) especially at Alouette Campground and Alouette Mountain, Gold Creek Corridor. Also present are *Black-headed Grosbeak, Pine Siskin* and *Purple Finch.*

A good day's birding in mid-May/June can produce 55-65 species.

Barred Owl

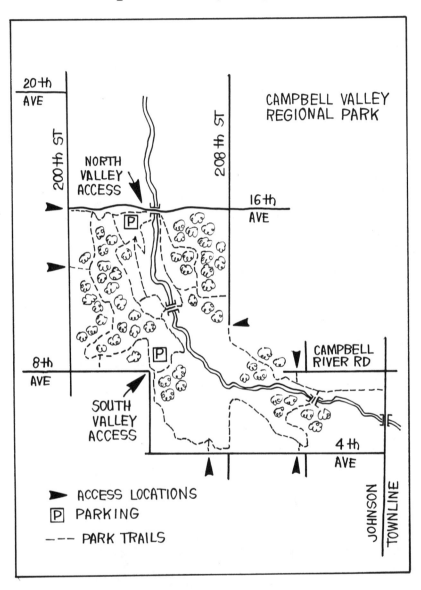

Campbell Valley Regional Park

CAMPBELL VALLEY REGIONAL PARK

Campbell Valley Regional Park is 50 km (31 mi) southeast of Vancouver. It is a 535 ha (1,320 ac) nature park in South Langley, operated by the Greater Vancouver Regional District. The park is a narrow valley approximately 2.5 km (1.5 mi) long, with the Little Campbell River meandering through its length.

Campbell Valley Park was opened as a Greater Vancouver Regional District Park in 1979. In the mid 1800's the Hudson Bay Company farmed and trapped in Campbell Valley. Pioneers moved into the area in the late 1800s using the land for cattle and hay production. In 1898 Alexander Annand moved into what is now the South Valley entrance area of Campbell Valley Park. He cleared the land for farming and built a small house. After two changes of ownership the property was acquired from Len Rowlatt in 1973 for the park. Old orchards and barns can be seen in many parts of Langley, all evidence of early homesteading. The Annand/Rolatt farmstead is preserved as a heritage site and visitors are welcome, but are asked to respect the privacy of the caretakers living in the farmhouse.

The area around Campbell Valley consists of farmland and a number of old gravel pits. The park itself is located in the Hazelmere Valley of South Langley. It extends south from 20th Avenue in the north, to 4th Avenue in the southeast from 200th Street to 216th Street. The valley floor is 300 - 700 m (990-2,310 ft) wide, and the steep sides are 30 m (99 ft) high. The east and west slopes of the valley are covered with deciduous and coniferous trees. Maple, western hemlock, Douglas fir, western red cedar and red alder being the more dominant species. On the floor of the valley, where it is damp and marshy, willow, black cottonwood, Pacific crabapple and hardhack take over. Interspersed with the trees are shrubs such as Saskatoon berry, ocean spray, false azalia, salal and hazelnut. In spring and summer the valley is full of the flowers of blackberry, salmonberry, and Nootka and little wild rose to name but a few. Wild flowers are everywhere, and the moist, boggy areas are full of mosses and ferns.

The Little Campbell River meanders sluggishly through the floodplain, where reeds, cattail, skunk cabbage, monkey flowers, water lilies and many other water loving plants grow. The lower part of the river supports fish such as trout and salmon. The Semiahmoo hatchery aids in the stocking of the river.

Equestrian sports are very active in the park, which includes an equestrian centre and extensive trails. While horses are not permitted on walking trails, hikers are allowed on horse trails. When walking on horse trails please be alert and courteous to approaching horses and riders, especially on curves and in dense woods. Horses can be easily spooked.

DIRECTIONS

Gas stations, stores, and restaurants can be found in the town of Langley and Brooks. At the North Valley entrance are parking facilities, picnic tables, drinking water and pit toilets. Walking trails start from here, including an excellent trail designed for wheelchairs (one toilet is also wheelchair accessible). At the south entrance there is parking, flush toilets, drinking water, a large picnic area and playing field. Here too is the Visitors Centre and a wildlife garden.

To reach Campbell Valley Park take Highway 1 (Trans Canada Highway) to the Langley 200th Street exit southbound. Go straight down 200th Street for 14.5 km (9.0 mi), and turn east on 16th Avenue for the North Valley entrance, located at the bottom of the hill on the right. This is less than one km after the turnoff. For the South Valley entrance proceed south on 200th Street and turn left on 8th Avenue. Or from Highway 99 South, take the 8th Avenue exit and drive 7.5 km (4.6 mi) to the south valley entrance. Wear suitable foot gear in fall, winter and spring. Some trails can become quite muddy in wet weather, especially horse trails.

BIRD SPECIES

Maps of the park are available at the notice boards at both the North and South entrances. Pick one up and you will find the trails quite easy to follow.

Little River Loop (approximately 2 km (1.2 mi))

Start at the North Valley entrance and take the trail to the left at the south end of the parking lot. It is also marked as a wheelchair trail. After walking approximately 160 m (528 ft) through the forest you will come to the first boardwalk across the marsh. The ***Black-capped Chickadee*** is common in the trees here, and ducks can be found to the north of the walkway, usually ***Mallard*** and in winter ***Green-winged Teal*** and ***American Wigeon.*** Continue on to the second and much longer boardwalk which crosses the main marsh through which the Little Campbell River meanders. In spring ***Common Snipe*** can be heard winnowing, ***Marsh Wren, Common Yellowthroat,*** and ***Violet-green, Tree and Barn swallows*** can all be seen. ***Pileated Woodpecker*** frequents the area at the east end of the boardwalk.

As you follow the trail it continues south with steep slopes on the left and marsh to the right. Many birds can be found on this section of trail: ***Bewick's Wren, Rufous-sided Towhee, Downy and Hairy Woodpeckers. Red-tailed Hawk*** and ***Great Horned Owl*** occasionally roost in the trees on the slope, sometimes very close to the path. In spring, watch for ***vireos, American Robin,*** and ***Red-breasted Nuthatch. Brown Creeper*** nests in dead trees along this area and can be seen collecting nesting material from cedars.

Because the slopes here face west they attract large numbers of passerines. In winter it is a sun trap and much warmer than other areas of the park and so birds tend to congregate here: *Varied Thrush,* and *Ruby-crowned and Golden-crowned Kinglets* are common.

The south end of the trail divides with one part continuing south, but turn right here to continue with the Little River loop trail. A boardwalk called the Listening bridge crosses back to the west side of the park. Take your time here. *Common Yellowthroat, Wilson's Warbler, Willow Flycatcher, Song Sparrow* and *Rufous Hummingbird* are common. Rarely *American Redstart* have been found here. There are benches halfway across on which to sit and enjoy a packed lunch or snack. Look up in spring and fall, you may see a *Turkey Vulture* circling above on an up current together with the more common *Red-tailed Hawk.*

After crossing the bridge follow the trail marked Little River loop, to the north (right). At first the trail is heavily treed with western redcedar, Douglas fir, alder, and broadleaf maple. *Brown Creeper, Ruffed Grouse* and in winter, *Fox Sparrow* may be seen. The

Brown Creeper

trail opens out to the Scenic Meadow where *Ring-necked Pheasant, Golden-crowned and White-crowned Sparrow, Orange-crowned Warbler* and *Blackheaded Grosbeak* can be found. Continue north to an area of tall and low shrubs. The honeysuckle here attracts *Rufous Hummingbird, American Goldfinch* and *Cedar Waxwing.* The rare *Ruby-throated Hummingbird* has also been seen. Towards the parking lot the shrubs and trees become more dense and are home to *Chestnut-backed Chickadee.* The trail has now returned to the 16th Avenue parking lot.

Alternate Trail Through Woods

Start at the south end of the North Valley parking lot taking the trail to the right of the notice board and toilets. Walk south approximately 170 m (560 ft), there take the turning to the right through dense fir - *Sharp-shinned Hawk* sometimes roost here. Some 250 m (825 ft) later turn left (south). This 600 m (1,980 ft) section passes through mixed forest and shrubs, an ideal place to find *Pacific -Slope Flycatcher, Western Wood-Peewe, Winter Wren* and *Dark-eyed Junco.* At the junction of the trail that comes in from the left continue south for another 300 m (990 ft). Here look for *Ruffed Grouse* and *Barred Owl.* The *owls* quite often roost in the trees and shrubs by the trail and a summer's evening is a good time to look. Sometimes the young can be heard giving a hissing call. Enjoy but please do not approach too close. The *owls* can be best seen using binoculars.

Continue south to a very large broadleaf maple with a prominent side limb. This tree is known as "The Hanging Tree". This local area of large trees on one side and more open terrain on the other, is particularly good for bird watching- *woodpeckers* in the tall trees and a variety of *warblers* in the shrubby more open areas. At this junction in the trail one can turn left and meet the Little River Loop trail, or continue south for about 600 m (1,980 ft) and arrive at the South (8th Avenue) parking lot and picnic area. Along this part of the trail there is a variety of habitat which supports an equally varied bird population, *Cedar Waxwing* and in winter, occasionally *Bohemian Waxwing* seem to like this location. One can now either go back to the 16th Avenue parking lot the way you came, or take an alternate route via a horse trail.

To return via the horse trail (length 3 km (1.9 mi), walk through the south entrance parking lot to the entrance and take the horse trail to the right. This trail first leads north and then travels west for a short distance. At about 1 km (0.6 mi) are two ponds,a good place to find *Great Blue Heron, Green-backed Heron, Hooded Merganser, Killdeer, Spotted Sandpiper,* and a large variety of *ducks* including *Ring-necked, teals* and *Common Goldeneye*. The trail meanders past the 3rd pond and in through mixed woods. Eventually one reaches 16th Avenue. Turn right (northeast), and you will come back to the 16th Avenue parking lot.

*Rufous
Hummingbird*

South Valley Trail (approximately 5 km (3.1 mi) round trip)

Drive to the 8th Avenue parking lot and park. Walk through to the Annand/Rowlatt farmstead areas and as you cross from one field to the next, look in the hedgerows for *Townsend's and Black throated Gray Warblers.* Also keep an eye open for *Sharp-shinned and Cooper's Hawk, Merlin* and *Peregrine Falcon.* In the second field, facing the homestead, turn left and take the Ravine Trail that starts in the north east corner. The trail leads into mixed woods. *Barred Owl* can sometimes be seen in early morning or late evening. As you walk through these woods look for *Downy and Hairy Woodpecker, Winter Wren* and *Ruffed Grouse.* After about 1 km (0.6 mi) you come to a sharp dip and a steep bank at the top of which one meets a horse trail. It is often muddy in the hollow but, with care, you can pick your way across. Turn left onto the horse trail and follow it as it winds across open ground - fields to the right and the river and wetlands below to the left. This open area is excellent for a variety of birds, raptors soaring above, *warblers* in the trees especially *Yellow-rumped, Black-throated Gray and Townsend's.* Look also for *American Goldfinch* and *Savannah Sparrow.* Keep walking southeast and follow the left hand trail which eventually leads down to the valley floor. Here the trail meets a shallow ford which the horses cross. If you look to your left as you approach the water you will see beaten paths through tall grasses which lead to a makeshift "bridge" across the narrow stream. After crossing the stream turn left onto the broad horse trail. This crosses a large flat area with lots of places to explore. The *Gray Catbird* has been seen in the shrubs to the right, and the trees to the left would be good for *flycatchers* and **Northern Flicker**. After exploring turn to the trail and continue to the bridge that crosses the river. Pause here to look for **Bewick's Wrens, Olive-sided Flycatcher, Rufous Hummingbird, Wilson's Warbler** and **Cliff Swallow.**

About 100 m (330 ft) after crossing the bridge the trail splits so turn left. Walking in a northwest direction the trail winds through trees and up the side of the east slope. Use caution on this section of trail, especially on weekends, because of the large number of horses and riders; please give way to horses. Birds to look for include **Swainson's and Hermit Thrushes, Steller's Jay** and in spring **Townsend's Solitaire**. At the top of the slope, before reaching the Equestrian Centre, look for a gap in the hedgerow on your left. Go through and cut across the field to the Little River Bowl. Take the steps that lead down to the old race track. The slopes are full of birds especially in spring and summer. Look for **House and Purple Finches, American Goldfinch, Song Sparrow** and **American Robin.** Keep right across the track, and exit through the gate.

Continue along the trail. The path leads across meadows with wooded slopes to the right, and marsh over to the left. Listen for **American Bittern** calling in spring. This section of trail eventually leads to the turnoff for the Listening Bridge. As you approach this turning there are large numbers of alder trees much favored by **Bushtit, Pine Siskin** and sometimes in winter, **Common Redpoll. Evening Grosbeak** flock to the broadleaf maples, and **Chestnut-backed Chickadee** like the conifers.

Take the Listening Bridge turnoff, cross the bridge, turn left again and return to the 8 Avenue (south) parking lot.

The main trails through the park have been listed. However there are a number of other entrances - two on 200th Street, two on 4th Avenue, one on 216th Avenue, and others.

There are 157 bird species listed for Campbell Valley Park including such rarities as **Great Gray Owl, Yellow-breasted Chat, Lazuli Bunting, American Redstart, Northern Goshawk, Calliope Hummingbird** and **Ruby-throated Hummingbird.**

Nine species of owls have been seen at one time or another including **Western Screech, Saw-whet, Great-horned, Barred, Northern Pygmy and Barn.** All except the **Northern Pygmy Owl** are known to nest in the park.

Take time to explore this beautiful park at all seasons, you never know what you might find!

CHECKLIST OF VANCOUVER BIRDS

Area covered: Greater Vancouver and vicinity from International Boundary (but including Point Roberts, Washington) north to 49° 35' N, west to Georgia Strait and Howe Sound, east to 122° 33' W (260th St. in Langley and Maple Ridge), but including all of Golden Ears Provincial Park.
Species covered: Only species recorded annually in the Vancouver area are included on this list; birds seen less than once per year are listed separately. Likewise, bars indicate only those periods in which species occur annually; e.g. although Great Egrets have wintered they occur annually only in fall.
Explanation of symbols
Abundance or frequency of occurrence in suitable habitat:

▬▬▬▬ Common to abundant (25 or more heard or seen each day)
▬▬▬ Fairly common (5 to 25 heard or seen each day)
——— Uncommon (0 to 5 heard or seen each day; more than 10 records per year)
——— Rare (often missed in a day; 1-10 records per year)
* Species known to have bred in checklist area

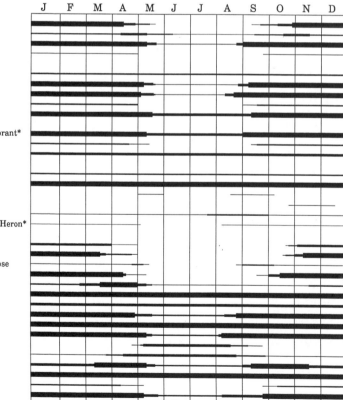

	J	F	M	A	M	J	J	A	S	O	N	D
Red-throated Loon												
Pacific Loon												
Common Loon												
Yellow-billed Loon												
Pied-billed Grebe*												
Horned Grebe												
Red-necked Grebe												
Eared Grebe												
Western Grebe*												
Double-crested Cormorant*												
Brandt's Cormorant												
Pelagic Cormorant*												
American Bittern*												
Great Blue Heron*												
Great Egret												
Cattle Egret												
Green-backed Heron*												
Black-crowned Night-Heron*												
Tundra Swan												
Trumpeter Swan												
Gr. White-fronted Goose												
Snow Goose												
Brant												
Canada Goose*												
Wood Duck*												
Green-winged Teal*												
Mallard*												
Northern Pintail*												
Blue-winged Teal*												
Cinnamon Teal*												
Northern Shoveler*												
Gadwall*												
Eurasian Wigeon												
American Wigeon*												

Checklist of Vancouver Birds

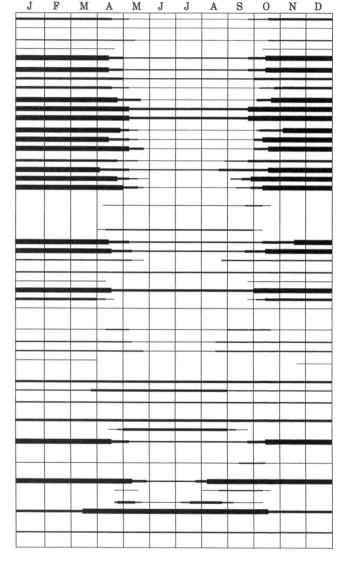

	J	F	M	A	M	J	J	A	S	O	N	D
Canvasback												
Redhead												
Ring-necked Duck												
Tufted Duck												
Greater Scaup												
Lesser Scaup												
Harlequin Duck*												
Oldsquaw												
Black Scoter												
Surf Scoter												
White-winged Scoter												
Common Goldeneye												
Barrow's Goldeneye												
Bufflehead												
Hooded Merganser*												
Common Merganser*												
Red-breasted Merganser												
Ruddy Duck*												
Turkey Vulture												
Osprey*												
Bald Eagle*												
Northern Harrier*												
Sharp-shinned Hawk*												
Cooper's Hawk*												
Northern Goshawk												
Red-tailed Hawk*												
Rough-legged Hawk												
Golden Eagle												
American Kestrel*												
Merlin*												
Peregrine Falcon												
Gyrfalcon												
Ring-necked Pheasant*												
Blue Grouse*												
Ruffed Grouse*												
Virginia Rail*												
Sora*												
American Coot*												
Sandhill Crane*												
Black-bellied Plover												
Lesser Golden-Plover												
Semipalmated Plover*												
Killdeer*												
Black Oystercatcher*												

Checklist of Vancouver Birds

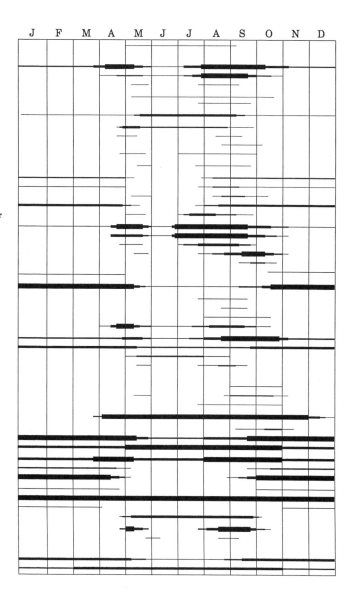

American Avocet*

Greater Yellowlegs
Lesser Yellowlegs
Solitary Sandpiper
Willet
Wandering Tattler
Spotted Sandpiper*
Whimbrel
Long-billed Curlew
Hudsonian Godwit
Marbled Godwit
Ruddy Turnstone
Black Turnstone
Surfbird
Red Knot
Sanderling
Semipalmated Sandpiper
Western Sandpiper
Least Sandpiper
Baird's Sandpiper
Pectoral Sandpiper
Sharp-tailed Sandpiper
Rock Sandpiper
Dunlin
Stilt Sandpiper
Buff-breasted Sandpiper
Ruff
Short-billed Dowitcher
Long-billed Dowitcher
Common Snipe*
Wilson's Phalarope
Red-necked Phalarope

Pomarine Jaeger
Parasitic Jaeger
Franklin's Gull
Bonaparte's Gull
Heermann's Gull
Mew Gull
Ring-billed Gull
California Gull
Herring Gull
Thayer's Gull
Western Gull
Glaucous-winged Gull*
Glaucous Gull
Caspian Tern*
Common Tern
Black Tern*

Common Murre
Pigeon Guillemot*

Checklist of Vancouver Birds

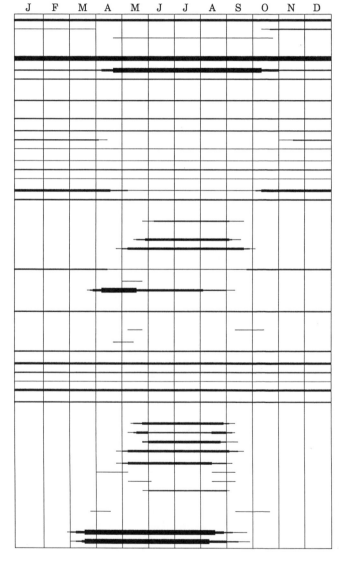

	J	F	M	A	M	J	J	A	S	O	N	D
Marbled Murrelet*												
Ancient Murrelet												
Rhinoceros Auklet												
Rock Dove*												
Band-tailed Pigeon*												
Mourning Dove*												
Barn Owl*												
Western Screech-Owl*												
Great Horned Owl*												
Snowy Owl												
Northern Pygmy-Owl*												
Spotted Owl*												
Barred Owl*												
Long-eared Owl*												
Short-eared Owl*												
Northern Saw-whet Owl*												
Common Nighthawk												
Black Swift												
Vaux's Swift												
Anna's Hummingbird												
Calliope Hummingbird												
Rufous Hummingbird*												
Belted Kingfisher*												
Lewis' Woodpecker*												
Red-naped Sapsucker*												
Red-breasted Sapsucker*												
Downy Woodpecker*												
Hairy Woodpecker*												
Three-toed Woodpecker*												
Northern Flicker*												
Pileated Woodpecker*												
Olive-sided Flycatcher*												
Western Wood-Pewee*												
Willow Flycatcher*												
Hammond's Flycatcher*												
Pacific-slope Flycatcher*												
Say's Phoebe												
Western Kingbird												
Eastern Kingbird*												
Horned Lark*												
Tree Swallow*												
Violet-green Swallow*												

Checklist of Vancouver Birds

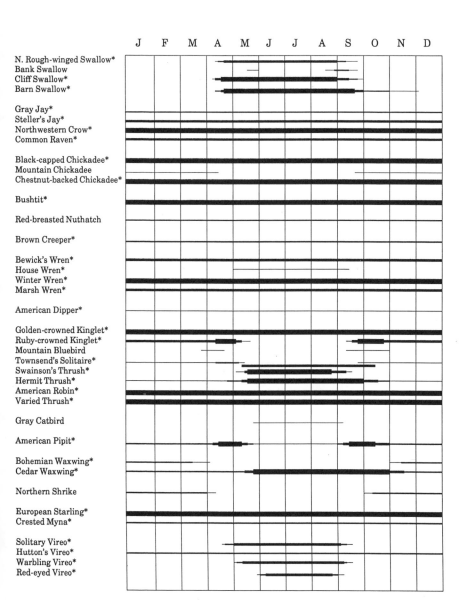

	J	F	M	A	M	J	J	A	S	O	N	D
N. Rough-winged Swallow*												
Bank Swallow												
Cliff Swallow*												
Barn Swallow*												
Gray Jay*												
Steller's Jay*												
Northwestern Crow*												
Common Raven*												
Black-capped Chickadee*												
Mountain Chickadee												
Chestnut-backed Chickadee*												
Bushtit*												
Red-breasted Nuthatch												
Brown Creeper*												
Bewick's Wren*												
House Wren*												
Winter Wren*												
Marsh Wren*												
American Dipper*												
Golden-crowned Kinglet*												
Ruby-crowned Kinglet*												
Mountain Bluebird												
Townsend's Solitaire*												
Swainson's Thrush*												
Hermit Thrush*												
American Robin*												
Varied Thrush*												
Gray Catbird												
American Pipit*												
Bohemian Waxwing*												
Cedar Waxwing*												
Northern Shrike												
European Starling*												
Crested Myna*												
Solitary Vireo*												
Hutton's Vireo*												
Warbling Vireo*												
Red-eyed Vireo*												

Checklist of Vancouver Birds

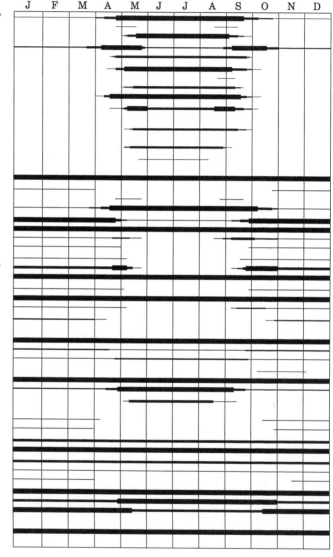

	J	F	M	A	M	J	J	A	S	O	N	D
Orange-crowned Warbler*												
Nashville Warbler												
Yellow Warbler*												
Yellow-rumped Warbler*												
Black-thr. Gray Warbler*												
Townsend's Warbler*												
Northern Waterthrush												
MacGillivray's Warbler*												
Common Yellowthroat*												
Wilson's Warbler*												
Western Tanager*												
Black-headed Grosbeak*												
Lazuli Bunting*												
Rufous-sided Towhee*												
American Tree Sparrow												
Chipping Sparrow*												
Savannah Sparrow*												
Fox Sparrow												
Song Sparrow*												
Lincoln's Sparrow												
Swamp Sparrow*												
White-throated Sparrow												
Golden-crowned Sparrow*												
White-crowned Sparrow*												
Harris' Sparrow												
Dark-eyed Junco*												
Lapland Longspur												
Snow Bunting												
Red-winged Blackbird*												
Western Meadowlark*												
Yellow-headed Blackbird*												
Rusty Blackbird												
Brewer's Blackbird*												
Brown-headed Cowbird*												
Northern Oriole*												
Rosy Finch												
Pine Grosbeak												
Purple Finch*												
House Finch*												
Red Crossbill*												
White-winged Crossbill												
Common Redpoll												
Pine Siskin*												
American Goldfinch*												
Evening Grosbeak*												
House Sparrow*												

Checklist of Vancouver Birds

CASUAL AND ACCIDENTAL SPECIES

Explanation of symbols:

Abundance or frequency of occurrence in suitable habitat:
ca = casual; 3 to many records, but seen on average less than once a year; somewhat out of normal range
acc =accidental; 1 to 2 records; usually far outside normal range

Seasonal Status:
W =winter
Sp =spring
S =summer
F =fall
T =transient in spring and fall

Other symbols:
sr =sight record; indicates casual and accidental species for which no specimens, photos, or tape recordings exist for the area, but for which acceptable field descriptions are on file with the VNHS.

Clark's Grebe	caW,sr	Common Moorhen	accSp&S
Sooty Shearwater	caF,sr	Snowy Plover	accSp
Short-tailed Shearwater	accF,sr	Black-necked Stilt	caSp
Fork-tailed Storm-Petrel	caF	Spotted Redshank	caT
American White Pelican	caS&F	Upland Sandpiper	caF
Brown Pelican	accSp&F,sr	Bristle-thighed Curlew	accSp,sr
Least Bittern	accS	Far Eastern Curlew	accF
Snowy Egret	accSp	Bar-tailed Godwit	caF
Ross' Goose	caW	Rufous-necked Stint	caS&F
Emperor Goose	caW	Little Stint	accS&F
Baikal Teal	accF	Temminck's Stint	accF&W
Garganey	accSp&S	White-rumped Sandpiper	accS&F,sr
King Eider	ca	Curlew Sandpiper	caF
Smew	caW	Spoonbill Sandpiper	accF
Black-shouldered Kite	caSp&S,sr	Red Phalarope	accS,caF
Prairie Falcon	caW	Long-tailed Jaeger	caF
Rock Ptarmigan	ca	South Polar Skua	caF,sr
White-tailed Ptarmigan	accF,sr	Little Gull	ca

Checklist of Vancouver Birds

Common Black-headed Gull	accF&W
Iceland Gull	caW
Slaty-backed Gull	accW
Black-legged Kittiwake	ca
Sabine's Gull	ca
Elegant Tern	accF
Arctic Tern	caT
Forster's Tern	caS&F,sr
Tufted Puffin	caS,sr
Northern Hawk Owl	caW
Burrowing Owl	ca
Great Gray Owl	caW
Common Poorwill	accF
White-throated Swift	accF
Ruby-throated Hummingbird	accSp&S,sr
Black-chinned Hummingbird	accSp,sr
Costa's Hummingbird	accSp
Yellow-bellied Sapsucker	accW,sr
Black-backed Woodpecker	accF,sr
Alder Flycatcher	accS,sr
Least Flycatcher	caS,sr
Dusky Flycatcher	caT,sr
Black Phoebe	accSp&F
Eastern Phoebe	accSp
Ash-throated Flycatcher	accS,caF
Eurasian Skylark	accW,sr
Purple Martin	caSp&S
Blue Jay	caW
Scrub Jay	accF
Clark's Nutcracker	ca
Black-billed Magpie	ca
Boreal Chickadee	accW,sr
White-breasted Nuthatch	caW,sr
Pygmy Nuthatch	accF,sr
Rock Wren	caW
Blue-gray Gnatcatcher	accF
Western Bluebird	ca
Veery	caSp&S,sr
Dusky Thrush	accW
Northern Mockingbird	ca
Sage Thrasher	accSp,sr
Brown Thrasher	accSp,sr
Yellow Wagtail	accF,sr
Black-backed Wagtail	accSp,sr
Red-throated Pipit	accF,sr
Loggerhead Shrike	caW
Philadelphia Vireo	accF
Tennessee Warbler	accSp&S, caF
Chestnut-sided Warbler	caS&F
Black-throated Green Warbler	accS,sr
Palm Warbler	caF,accW
Black-and-white Warbler	ca,sr
American Redstart	caS&F
Canada Warbler	accSp,sr
Ovenbird	accSp,sr
Painted Redstart	accF,sr
Yellow-breasted Chat	caS
Indigo Bunting	accS
Clay-colored Sparrow	acc
Brewer's Sparrow	accSp&F
Vesper Sparrow	ca
Lark Sparrow	caT,sr
Black-throated Sparrow	caSp&S
Sage Sparrow	accSp&F
Lark Bunting	caF
Baird's Sparrow	accSp&S,sr
Grasshopper Sparrow	accS&F
Sharp-tailed Sparrow	accF,sr
Smith's Longspur	accF,sr
Chestnut-collared Longspur	accS,sr
Bobolink	caSp&S
Common Grackle	accSp&S
Brambling	caF&W
Cassin's Finch	caT
Lesser Goldfinch	accF,sr

SELECTED LIST OF BIRD SPECIES FOUND IN THE VANCOUVER AREA

There are two main approaches which can be followed in a bird-watching guide. The first approach emphasizes a bird-watching locality: "What species of birds can I expect to find in Area X?" This approach has been followed in this guide. The second approach emphasizes the particular bird species: "Where can I find species X?". This approach, which is especially useful to visitors from other areas, is the subject of this section.

Many of the bird species found in the Vancouver area are common, not only in this area, but over a large part of North America. No special directions are needed to find these birds, because the observer is likely to find them in a very short time anyway. However, there is a long list of species which are either uncommon or rare locally (and thus sought after by local birdwatchers), or which may be common locally, but which are rare or absent in much of the U.S. and Canada (and hence sought after by visiting birders). This list is therefore an attempt to combine two lists of "wanted species": those wanted by Vancouver-area birders, and those wanted by visiting birders. The choice of species included is subjective, but it does include all the species about which local bird experts are asked most frequently.

Casual and accidental species (those occurring, on average, less than once a year in the Vancouver area) are not included in this list because they are too unpredictable. In any case, they are nearly always mentioned on the Vancouver Natural History Society's taped Rare Bird Alert.

Pacific Loon

This species, although common around Victoria, is uncommon at best around Vancouver (mainly from Oct. to Apr.); it prefers deep water and strong tidal currents, and is rarely seen in shallow water, unlike other loons. It is much more gregarious than other loons. Point Roberts is by far the best locality. Large flocks occur off the Reifel Bird Sanctuary (Fraser River mouth) in late Apr. and early May, but usually too far off for good viewing. If you cannot find this bird around Vancouver, you can be nearly sure of seeing large flocks in Active Pass, on the Vancouver-Victoria ferry route, from fall through late spring.

Yellow-billed Loon

Very rare in winter (mainly Oct. to early May), but usually reported several times a year. Point Roberts is easily the most frequent locality; also possible at Iona Island, Jericho Park, Stanley Park, Ambleside Park, Lighthouse Park, and localities around Boundary Bay. Identification can be tricky, especially immatures; exercise caution.

Red-necked Grebe

Fairly common from early fall (late Aug.) to spring (early May). Widely distributed, but best localities include Point Roberts, Tsawwassen and Roberts Bank jetties, Stanley Park, and (especially in fall), Blackie Spit and the foot of ll2th Street on Boundary Bay.

Brandt's Cormorant Like the Pacific Loon, this bird prefers deep water, and can reliably be found (Sept. to Apr.) in large flocks in Active Pass. In the Vancouver area proper, the two most reliable spots (Oct. to Apr.) are the Grebe Islets off Lighthouse Park and the Burnaby Shoal channel marker off Brockton Point in Stanley Park. A powerful telescope is helpful at both these spots. Large flocks often appear off Point Roberts in late fall (Oct. to Dec.), but are irregular in occurrence.

American Bittern An uncommon resident, bordering on rare. In summer, the best area is the Pitt Wildlife Management Area, along Rennie Road or Middleton Road, where birds can be heard "pumping" near sunrise or sunset. In winter, Reifel Bird Sanctuary is the best spot; from 1-10 bitterns winter, and sometimes occur close to the dikes during high tides. Other regular but less frequent localities include Addington Marsh and Campbell Valley Regional Park (summer), Sea Island and Brunswick Point (winter).

Green-backed Heron Uncommon in summer, very rare in winter; most frequent in Aug. and Sept., when northward-dispersing juveniles augment the small breeding population. Possible almost anywhere along lowland streams and sloughs, but the best spots include Pitt Meadows, Addington Marsh\Minnekhada Regional Park, Burnaby Lake Regional Park, Campbell Valley Regional Park, Jericho Park, and Ambleside Park.

Black-crowned Night-Heron From 3-6 birds winter regularly (Sept. to May) at the Reifel Bird Sanctuary, where they are usually easy to see in their daytime roost in trees bordering Fuller Slough. This is the only reliable spot for this species in B.C.

Trumpeter Swan Common in winter, with numbers increasing rapidly in the last 10 years. Recently, up to 500 have wintered at Brunswick Point and Westham and Reifel Islands, and are most easily seen along the shoreline there or along the Lulu Island West Dike, or feeding in fields along Westham Island Road. The south end of Pitt Lake (see under Pitt Meadows) also has a wintering flock of about 100 birds. Beware of confusion with Tundra Swan, which also winters in some numbers (voice is the best distinction); however, most of the Tundra Swans usually winter in a separate flock (about 100 birds) between Ladner and Deas Island Regional Park in Delta.

Brant Uncommon in winter, common or even abundant in spring. From 30-200 birds usually winter in Boundary Bay, and are best seen from the shoreline of Boundary Bay Regional Park. Flocks of up to 1000 or more are present in spring (late Feb. to early May), mainly near eelgrass beds in Boundary Bay and Roberts Bank. Best viewing localities include the White Rock waterfront, Boundary Bay Regional Park, Point Roberts (mainly flying by), and the Tsawwassen and Roberts Bank jetties.

Eurasian Wigeon Increasingly numerous in recent years; although females are usually unidentifiable, a ratio of 1 male Eurasian Wigeon to 100 American Wigeon is typical. Widespread; can be found in winter (late Sept. to late Apr.) anywhere that American Wigeon are found, but best spots include Reifel Bird Sanctuary, Roberts Bank jetty, Blackie Spit, and Beach Grove.

Ring-necked Duck Prefers freshwater ponds and lakes; surprisingly scarce in the Vancouver area. In winter (late Sept. to early May) one or two are usually on Lost Lagoon, Stanley Park, but more frequent at Pitt Meadows and Minnekhada Park. One or a few birds summer regularly at Iona Island.

Tufted Duck
First recorded in 1961, but now seen several times almost every winter (late Sept. to early May), with individuals often remaining for weeks. Usually with scaup, and most often on fresh water. The most frequent localities are Stanley Park (usually Lost Lagoon) and Iona Island. Females, as well as males, are readily identifiable and should be watched for.

Harlequin Duck
Uncommon to fairly common; sizable numbers of non-breeders remain all summer, so can usually be seen year-round at its favourite localities. The best spots are Point Roberts and Ambleside Park; smaller numbers (less than 10) can usually be found at Lighthouse Park, Stanley Park (near Ferguson Point) and Maplewood Flats.

Oldsquaw
Fairly common in winter (early Oct. to early May), usually in salt water well offshore. The waters off Point Roberts usually have the largest numbers. Other consistent localities include Stanley Park, Jericho Park, Iona Island south jetty, the Roberts Bank and Tsawwassen jetties, Boundary Bay Regional Park, and White Rock.

Barrow's Goldeneye
Abundant in winter, but often a new bird for visiting birders. Usually off rocky shorelines, where it feeds in mixed flocks of hundreds with Surf Scoters. Most numerous at Stanley Park, Lighthouse Park, Ambleside Park, or anywhere along shorelines of Burrard Inlet, English Bay, and Howe Sound. Generally rare in the Fraser Delta and Boundary Bay.

Bald Eagle
Uncommon in summer, with perhaps 10-12 breeding pairs in the area; breeding localities include Stanley Park, Lighthouse Park, Reifel Island (the Alaksen Natl. Wildlife Area) and Point Roberts. In winter, ubiquitous, with sizable numbers occurring around Boundary Bay and the Fraser River mouth at the Reifel Bird Sanctuary (not unusual to see 20-40 birds at once in either area). Outside the immediate Vancouver area, gatherings of up to several hundred birds can be seen in early winter (Nov. to early Feb.) along salmon spawning streams like the lower Squamish and Harrison Rivers.

Rough-legged Hawk
Fairly common in winter (Oct. to Apr.), especially in farmlands of the Fraser Delta area, where they often outnumber Red-tailed Hawks. Best localities include the north side of Boundary Bay, especially near the Boundary Bay airport, Sea and Iona Islands, Westham Island, fields east of Roberts Bank, Boundary Bay Regional Park, and Pitt Meadows.

Merlin
Very rare in summer, uncommon in winter (late Aug. to early May). As numerous here in winter as it is anywhere in North America, with at least 20-30 birds probably wintering in the area. Likely to be seen almost anywhere in open areas, and also seen regularly if less often in residential areas in forest edges. You will probably find this bird at Iona Island or the Reifel Bird Sanctuary as it chases away a flock of shorebirds that you very much wanted to study more closely.

Peregrine Falcon
Uncommon in winter (late Aug. to early May), with possibly 12-20 birds wintering in the area, mostly of the dark subspecies pealei. In recent years, one or two non-breeding birds have also been seen regularly in summer in the Fraser Delta. The Peregrine prefers shorelines much more than the Merlin, and preys largely on shorebirds (e.g. Dunlin) and small ducks (e.g. Green-winged Teal). Best localities include Sea and Iona Islands, Reifel Bird Sanctuary, Brunswick Point, and the entire shoreline of Boundary Bay. Like the Merlin, it has an annoying habit of chasing off a flock of shorebirds just when you thought you had spotted something rare.

Gyrfalcon

Very rare in winter (generally Nov. to Mar.); only two or three sightings in some winters, but other years with 3 or 4 birds present for weeks at a time. Generally much more wide-ranging than the Peregrine; may be reported at one spot one day, and 10 km away the next day. Best localities include Westham and Reifel Islands, Sea and Iona Islands, Brunswick Point and fields east of Roberts Bank, and fields on the north side of Boundary Bay. Hunts inland more often than the Peregrine Falcon.

Blue Grouse

Easy to find when males are hooting (late Mar. to early Aug.), harder in late summer, nearly impossible in winter, when birds winter in mountain conifer forests. Easily found in spring and in summer at Mount Seymour and Cypress Provincial Parks, but hooting males are often very hard to see in the treetops. From 2-4 males hoot each year in Lighthouse Park, and are even harder to see. Most easily seen from June through August, when females with young are often seen on the road (early morning is best!) as one drives up the Mt. Seymour or Cypress access roads.

Sandhill Crane

A remnant population of 2-3 pairs breeds in Pitt Meadows, and birds can be seen or heard from late Mar. to Sept. from Rennie Road in the Pitt Wildlife Management Area or fields just to the south. At least one pair still attempts to breed in Burns Bog, Delta, and can often be seen near 68th Street, south of River Road in Delta. Since 1980, from 1-3 birds have often wintered in this same area along 68th Street. Small concentrations of up to 30 birds can also be seen in Sept. and Oct. in fields near 68th Street and 60th Avenue, Delta.

Lesser Golden-Plover

A rare migrant in spring (late Apr.-early May), uncommon in fall (late Aug.- late Oct.). Most spring records are along the shores of Boundary Bay or in fields north of the bay. In fall, more widespread. One to 3 can often be found among the large flocks of Black-bellied Plovers near the foot of ll2th Street on Boundary Bay. However, most often found away from water, on airports, golf courses, turf farms. Likely spots include Sea and Iona Islands, Westham Island, and the turf farm on 72nd Street, Delta. Both the dominica and fulva forms are found: dominica seems to be commoner in Aug. and Sept., and fulva in Oct.

Black Oystercatcher

This bird has occurred regularly only since 1974. The best spot is the Grebe Islets off Lighthouse Park (best viewed from Kloochman Park), where oystercatchers nest every year and are seen year-round. Other nearby feeding localities include the mouth of Cypress Creek, the entrance to Eagle Harbour, and Whytecliff Park, all in West Vancouver. Since 1990, a little more widespread, and also seen regularly at Ferguson Point, Stanley Park, and on the Tsawwassen ferry jetty. Much more common in the Victoria area than around Vancouver.

American Avocet

Rare in summer (mainly Apr. to Aug.), seen most years but not every year. In 3 recent years, they have attempted nesting at Serpentine Fen. Other likely spots include Iona Island and Westham and Reifel Islands.

Whimbrel

A fairly common spring migrant, less common in summer, uncommon in fall. The most reliable spot is Gilbert Beach, along Dyke Road on the south side of Lulu Island. In late Apr. and early May, up to 100 Whimbrel are consistently found here at low tide, or in nearby fields at high tide. Semiahmoo Bay near White Rock (mostly south of the International Border) is also a spring concentration point; birds from this area sometimes feed at high tide in Hazelmere Valley (along 8th Avenue) in Surrey. Iona Island is also a good spot in spring. In July and August, up to 20 are often seen at Blackie Spit, and in some years, one or two have wintered there.

Long-billed Curlew

Very rare migrant, mainly in spring. Most often reported from Sea and Iona Islands. Other possible localities are Westham and Reifel Islands, the Roberts Bank jetty, Blackie Spit, and Pitt Meadows.

Hudsonian Godwit

A very rare fall migrant (mainly Aug. to Oct.), casual in spring, but seen nearly every year. When one shows up, it often stays for weeks. Most records have been from Iona Island, the Reifel Bird Sanctuary, Boundary Bay (especially the foot of ll2th Street), and Blackie Spit.

Marbled Godwit

Not quite so rare as the Hudsonian Godwit, but usually seen as singles. Most often reported in Apr. and May, but possible any month of the year. The most likely localities are Blackie Spit and the foot of ll2th Street; Iona Island and the Roberts Bank jetty are also worth checking.

Surfbird

Nearly always seen on rocky, wave-swept shorelines with Black Turnstones. Present from late July to early May, but more numerous in fall. The best areas are the islands and shorelines of Howe Sound, including the Grebe Islets, Lighthouse Park, islands off Eagle Harbour, and Whytecliff Park. A powerful telescope is helpful for scanning distant islands. The mouth of Cypress Creek, West Vancouver, is a regular feeding spot at low tide which is easily accessible. Flocks sometimes seen on jetties such as the Iona Island south jetty and Tsawwassen jetty, but irregular in occurrence there.

Red Knot

Rare migrant; most records in May, Aug., and Sept. Often found among flocks of Black-bellied Plovers, the best spot is near the foot of ll2th Street on Boundary Bay. Possible anywhere else around Boundary Bay, and there are also many records from Iona Island.

Sharp-tailed Sandpiper

This bird is more consistently found around Vancouver than anywhere else in North America south of Alaska. It is a rare but regular fall migrant, usually found with flocks of Pectoral Sandpipers, from which it should be distinguished with care. (Nearly all records of Sharp-tails are of juveniles.) Likely to be found anytime between about Sept. 15 and Oct. 31; the first week of Oct. is best. Most years, it is possible to find 3-5 in a day, although up to 14 have been seen at once, and in other years, there have been only 3-4 sightings. Nearly all sightings are from the Reifel Bird Sanctuary or the Iona Island sewage ponds, which probably rate equally as good Sharp-tail localities.

Rock Sandpiper

Found in the same localities as Surfbird (see under that species), but in much smaller numbers (usually less than 10) and for a shorter time period (Oct. to Apr.). It can be hard to pick out this bird among flocks of Surf birds and Black Turnstones; a good spotting scope is essential. If you cannot find it around Vancouver, a reliable spot (at low tide) is Mission Point (the mouth of Chapman Creek), about 3 km east of Sechelt, which is easily reached by ferry from West Vancouver (Horseshoe Bay).

Stilt Sandpiper

A rare but regular fall migrant, mainly in late Aug. and Sept. The best localities are Iona Island, the Reifel Bird Sanctuary, and the tidal lagoon at Beach Grove.

Buff-breasted Sandpiper

A rare fall migrant (mainly late Aug. and Sept.), seen most but not all years, singly or in small flocks. Likes the same places as Lesser Golden-Plovers, i.e., airports, turf farms, and other short-grass areas. The most likely localities are fields north of Boundary Bay (especially the turf farm on the west side of 72nd Street, Delta), Sea and Iona Islands, and Westham Island.

Ruff   Although first recorded in 1971, it is now seen every year, with 1 to 4 records each year. Most records are from late July through Oct., but there are a few spring records as well. The great majority of records are from the Iona Island sewage ponds and the Reifel Bird Sanctuary.

Parasitic Jaeger   A very rare spring migrant (usually late May), uncommon in fall (late Aug. to mid-Nov.). Point Roberts is by far the best spot, especially Lighthouse Marine Park, at the southwest corner of the point; from 4-6 birds can often be seen there in a couple of hours. Other regular spots include Stanley Park (mainly the English Bay side), Jericho Park/Spanish Banks , the Iona Island south jetty, the Tsawwassen jetty, and the shores of Boundary Bay.

Franklin's Gull   Rare in fall (late July to early Nov.), casual at any other time of year. The Iona Island sewage ponds are the best spot. Possible wherever there are Bonaparte's Gulls; other localities with repeated sightings include Maplewood Flats, Stanley Park, Point Roberts, Beach Grove, and Blackie Spit and the crab pier at Jericho Park.

Heermann's Gull   Vancouver is at the northern end of this species' range. It is seen only during fall dispersal (late Aug. or Sept. through Nov.), and nearly all records are from Point Roberts, although it is also possible at (or just off) the Tsawwassen ferry terminal. Numbers fluctuate greatly, with peak counts in the hundreds some years, and less than 10 in others. Look for them in mixed-species feeding flocks off Lighthouse Marine Park at Point Roberts, or resting on the beach at Lily Point (the southeast tip of Point Roberts).

Thayer's Gull   Easily found from mid-Sept. through April; this is the third commonest gull species wintering in the Vancouver area, after Glaucous-winged and Mew Gulls. For comparison, average Vancouver Christmas Count totals are 9000 Glaucous-winged, 3600 Mew, and 500 Thayer's Gulls. There are almost always some Thayer's Gulls along the shorelines of Iona and Sea Islands, or in the daytime gull roost on islands just above the Capilano River mouth, next to Ambleside Park. On rainy days, check any grassy park or playing field in Vancouver or Richmond, where a few Thayer's Gulls will be hunting for worms along with Glaucous-wings and Mews. Also, check the huge flocks of loafing gulls which spent much of the day in fields near the Burns Bog landfill in Delta (look for them along Burns Drive, 68th Street, or Highway 10 between 72nd Street and 96th Street); there are always many Thayer's in these flocks. Distinguish with care from Herring Gulls, which are outnumbered at least 20 to 1 by Thayer's.

Western Gull   Rare in winter (mainly Oct. to Apr.) Most easily found by checking gull flocks near the Burns Bog landfill (see under Thayer's Gull). Can also be found at Stanley Park, Jericho Park, or any other place frequented by many Glaucous-winged Gulls. Adults are readily identified; first-year to third-year birds are trickier. However, Western X Glaucous-winged Gull intergrades outnumber pure Western Gulls by 5 or 10 to 1. Any Western-type gull which lacks jet-black wingtips, or other typical Western Gull field marks, is best considered an intergrade.

Glaucous Gull   Rare in winter (mainly Nov. to Mar.). Adult plumaged birds are very rare; most are second or third winter birds, with nearly white plumage, which are easy to identify. This gull, more than any other, prefers the Burns Bog landfill in Delta, which is not open to birders. However, a Glaucous Gull can often be found by scanning nearby roosting gull flocks (see localities under Thayer's Gull) or checking log booms on the Fraser River just east of Deas Island Regional Park, Delta.

Pigeon Guillemot   In summer, a breeding colony occupies the cliffs below Prospect Point in Stanley Park and can be seen feeding nearby in Burrard Inlet. They also nest on islands off Lighthouse Park, and can be seen there year-round. Less numerous in winter, but regularly seen at Point Roberts, Lighthouse Park, Stanley Park, and Ambleside Park.

Marbled Murrelet   Fairly common year-round: good spots include Point Roberts, Stanley Park, Lighthouse Park, Ambleside Park, Maplewood Flats. Generally common in coastal inlets like Howe Sound and Burrard Inlet, scarce in shallow waters of the Fraser Delta and Boundary Bay. Especially in winter, concentrations are highly mobile; there may be 40 birds in an area one day, none the next day.

Ancient Murrelet   Uncommon in winter (Oct. to Apr.), but most reports are in Oct. and Nov. Much more gregarious than the Marbled Murrelet; tends to feed farther offshore, in tight flocks. Nearly all sightings are from Point Roberts; some years, there may be only 2-3 sightings. Much commoner around Victoria than around Vancouver.

Rhinoceros Auklet   Rare in summer (Apr. to Nov.); most frequent in late summer and fall, but rarely more than 3-4 birds at once. Most readily seen at Point Roberts (Lighthouse Marine Park); also possible off the Tsawwassen and Iona Island jetties, Lighthouse Park, Stanley Park (English Bay side). Surprisingly rare at Vancouver, considering that there is a huge breeding colony near Sequim, Washington, and the bird is abundant in summer off the Victoria waterfront.

Barn Owl   Uncommon resident, mainly in farmland in the Fraser Delta; less numerous in eastern parts of the Vancouver area. Most easily found by entering occupied barns (with owner's permission!) in the daytime; can also be found by scanning telephone poles and fence posts on Sea and Westham Islands at night with a flashlight. Best localities include Sea and Iona Islands, Westham Island, Boundary Bay, Beach Grove, and Pitt Meadows.

Western Screech-Owl   Uncommon resident in forested areas throughout. Most vocal from Feb. through May, but can be prodded into vocalizing at any time of year with the help of tape-recorded calls. Consistent localities include Mount Seymour Provincial Park (near park entrance), Lynn Canyon Park (North Vancouver), Pacific Spirit Regional Park, Point Roberts, and Campbell Valley Regional Park.

Snowy Owl   Uncommon winter resident (mainly Nov. to Mar.). "Flight years" occur every 3-4 years, when populations of lemmings on the Alaskan breeding grounds collapse; in those years, from 10 to (exceptionally!) more than 100 may winter in the area. At least one or two are present every winter, however. Snowy Owls like open country, especially along shorelines, and are often seen on the Iona Island and Roberts Bank jetties. The most reliable spot by far is the foot of 72nd Street on Boundary Bay (especially on logs outside the dike, but often in fields along the road as well). Anywhere else along the shoreline of Boundary Bay is worth checking, as are Sea and Iona Islands, Reifel and Westham Islands, and Brunswick Point.

Northern Pygmy-Owl   Rare resident. Found almost exclusively in the North Shore Mountains and Pitt Meadows; unrecorded in the Fraser Delta. Most often seen in winter (Oct. to Apr.), but can be found in summer also. Best bets are Mt. Seymour and Cypress Parks (scan the treetops while driving up or down the access roads); also possible, but less likely, at Lighthouse Park and Pitt Meadows.

Spotted Owl   Very rare resident in old-growth conifer forest in the Capilano River and Seymour River watersheds on the North Shore. These areas are unfortunately closed to public access; more accessible locations in B.C. outside the Vancouver area are near Lillooet Lake, Chilliwack Lake, and the Skagit River valley.

Long-eared Owl   Rare resident, seen mainly in the Fraser Delta area in winter. Careful checking of deciduous thickets in such areas as Sea Island, Lulu Island west dike, Reifel and Westham Islands, Brunswick Point, and fields north of Boundary Bay may reveal one or two of these birds. Staff at the Reifel Bird Sanctuary may be able to direct you to one of these birds.

Northern Saw-whet Owl   Uncommon resident, usually found in conifers, more frequent in winter (near sea level, at least). In spring, may respond to tapes in breeding localities such as Pacific Spirit Park, Point Roberts, Campbell Valley Regional Park. In winter, can be found by careful searching of trees in places like the Reifel Bird Sanctuary and Sea Island From one to four usually winter at Reifel Island, and staff at the Sanctuary may be able to direct you to one (no photographers, please!).

Black Swift   Fairly common in summer (mid-May to mid-Sept.). Probably nest in coastal mountains; can be seen in small numbers anytime at Cypress and Mount Seymour Provincial Parks or near Pitt Lake. In lowland areas, seen occasionally in large flocks during inclement weather with low-hanging clouds (movements are weather-related). It can show up almost anywhere, so keep alert in cloudy weather.

Vaux's Swift   Fairly common in summer (late Apr. to mid-Sept.). Does not wander as widely as Black Swift; in summer, most often seen in North and West Vancouver, Stanley Park, and Pitt Meadows. Possible anywhere in spring and fall migration.

Anna's Hummingbird   Rare in summer, uncommon in winter; gradually increasing in numbers since it was first recorded about 1970. Seen most often in winter (Oct.-Apr.), when it usually stays close to hummingbird feeders. Found mainly in residential areas; rarely seen away from houses, except at Lighthouse Park, where it may breed. Most often recorded from West Vancouver, the Kerrisdale area of Vancouver (south of 33rd Avenue and west of Granville Street), and White Rock. Best found by obtaining current addresses where birds are regularly visiting feeders; try phoning people whose phone numbers are listed on the Rare Bird Alert tape for help.

Red-breasted Sapsucker   Uncommon resident, usually found in dense conifer forest. Most common at altitudes above 800 metres. Best localities are Mount Seymour and Cypress Provincial Parks, Lighthouse Park, Pitt Meadows, and Golden Ears Provincial Park (nests in all 5 areas). Also possible, mainly in winter, in Stanley Park, Pacific Spirit Regional Park, and Point Roberts. A partial altitudinal migrant, but usually seen most often in the mountains even in winter.

Three-toed Woodpecker   Rare resident; usually reported only 1-4 times a year. The only consistent locality is Cypress Provincial Park, occasionally along the Yew Lake trail, but more often along the Howe Sound Crest Trail, which involves fairly strenuous hiking. Much easier to find in Manning Provincial Park and other areas well to the east of Vancouver.

Hammond's Flycatcher
Fairly common in summer (mid-Apr, to mid-Sept.), generally in heavy conifer forest and mixed forest at lower altitudes. Most easily found at Mount Seymour Provincial Park (near entrance), Lighthouse Park, Minnekhada Regional Park, Golden Ears Provincial Park; possible in any wooded area during migration. Identification is simplified by the fact that the Dusky Flycatcher, with which Hammond's is often confused, does not breed around Vancouver and is an extremely rare migrant.

Pacific-Slope Flycatcher
Fairly common in summer (late Apr. to mid-Sept.), although much more numerous than Hammond's, and occurs at higher altitudes (up to 1200 m or more). Prefers conifer forest with a deciduous understory (e.g. vine maple), but breeds in most forested areas around Vancouver. The distinction between this species and Cordilleran Flycatcher may not be valid in B.C., as interior populations seem intermediate in many respects.

Eastern Kingbird
Uncommon in summer (late May to early Sept.). Found regularly only in the Pitt Wildlife Management area (e.g. at Grant Narrows and along Rennie Road), where a few pairs nest every year. This is one of the several species known locally as "Pitt Meadows specialties". Finding one elsewhere is pure luck, although there are records from a number of other localities.

Chestnut-backed Chickadee
Abundant resident. This is one of the commonest birds in conifer forest throughout the region. In winter, it also occurs to some extent in adjacent deciduous woods when feeding in mixed flocks with Golden-crowned Kinglets and Black-capped Chickadees. Very rare in the Fraser Delta. Good places to see this bird include (but are not limited to) Mount Seymour and Cypress Provincial Parks, Lighthouse Park, Pitt Meadows, Golden Ears Provincial Park, Pacific Spirit Regional Park, and Point Roberts.

Bushtit
Common resident, found mainly in residential areas, hedgerows, woodlots, and forest edges, but not in extensive forest areas. Less numerous on the North Shore. Usually in large flocks from August to March. Good places to look include Jericho Park, Pacific Spirit Regional Park (edges), Queen Elizabeth Park, Sea Island, Reifel Bird Sanctuary, Point Roberts, Burnaby Lake Regional Park, Campbell Valley Regional Park, and Pitt Meadows.

Bewick's Wren
Fairly common resident, found in hedgerows, brush, woodlots, and forest edges and openings. Although not migratory, it can be harder to find in winter, when it is not very vocal. Good spots to find it include Ambleside Park, Stanley Park, Jericho Park, Pacific Spirit Park, Reifel Bird Sanctuary, Point Roberts, Burnaby Lake Regional Park, Campbell Valley Regional Park, and Pitt Meadows.

Townsend's Solitaire
Rare resident, uncommon spring migrant. Most easily found in April and early May, when small numbers pass through every year. The most reliable spot is Queen Elizabeth Park, but possible almost anywhere, especially in North and West Vancouver and Pitt Meadows. Rare but regular in winter; the most likely spot again is Queen Elizabeth Park, and it is worth searching residential areas of North and West Vancouver, especially those farthest up the mountains. Very rare in summer in the North Shore mountains; not seen every year in summer.

Varied Thrush

Fairly common in summer, common in winter. Breeds in heavy conifer forest, occasionally down to sea level, but most commonly above 700 metres. In summer, best found in Cypress, Mount Seymour, and Golden Ears Provincial Parks, where it is common (but shy and sometimes hard to see). In winter, still prefers conifer forest, but can be found in almost any wooded area (even small woodlots) and in residential areas, especially when there is heavy snow in the mountains. Numbers can vary by a factor of 10 between one winter and the next.

Gray Catbird

Rare in summer (late May to early Sept.). This is a "Pitt Meadows specialty", found regularly only in the Pitt Wildlife Management Area. The best spots are the wooded dyke leading southeast from Grant Narrows, and brushy areas along Rannie Road about 2 km south of Grant Narrows. Fewer than 5 pairs breed in the Vancouver area most years. Possible in several other locations, but only Pitt Meadows has been consistent.

Northern Shrike

Uncommon in winter (early Oct. to mid-Apr.). Found in open country, usually on telephone wires or in treetops. The most likely spots include Sea and Iona Islands, Reifel and Westham Island, Brunswick Point to Roberts Bank, the Boundary Bay dikes and adjacent fields, and Pitt Meadows.

Crested Myna

This species, introduced to Vancouver from Asia in the 1890s and once boasting a population of thousands of birds, is probably reduced to fewer than 100 birds now. It is essentially confined to the City of Vancouver and built-up areas of Lulu Island in Richmond, although it once ranged more widely. Good localities to look include the vicinity of 49th Ave. and Fraser St., 70th Ave. and Oak Street, 70th Avenue and Granville Street, or 4th Avenue and MacDonald Street in Vancouver. If you have trouble finding them, try phoning one of the persons whose phone number is listed on the Rare Bird Alert tape. Mynas usually remain in pairs all year, and often flock with Starlings in winter. They are thoroughly urban birds, and are often seen along main streets; look for them sitting on chimneytops, feeding on lawns, or looking for scraps around fast-food restaurants. They are noisy, and are often heard before they are seen.

Hutton's Vireo

Uncommon resident, preferring second-growth deciduous and mixed woods. They can be hard to find in winter, when they are usually silent, and accompany flocks of kinglets and chickadees. A Hutton's Vireo seen briefly can be easily mistaken for a Ruby-crowned Kinglet. From February to July, easily located by its persistent, monotonous song. Most easily found in wooded areas of Point Roberts; also regular at Lighthouse Park, Stanley Park, Pacific Spirit Regional Park, Burnaby Lake Regional Park, Campbell Valley Regional Park, and Pitt Meadows.

Black-throated Gray Warbler

Fairly common in summer (late Apr. to late Sept.), mainly in broadleaf forest and second-growth conifer forest at low altitudes. Generally not found above 600 m altitude. The best spots include Lighthouse Park, Stanley Park, Pacific Spirit Regional Park, Point Roberts, Campbell Valley Regional Park, Minnekhada Regional Park, Golden Ears Provincial Park, and Pitt Meadows.

Townsend's Warbler

Common in summer (late Apr. to early Oct.), mainly in mountain conifer forests; breeds in much smaller numbers down to sea level where there are old-growth forests (e.g. Lighthouse Park). The best localities in summer are Cypress, Mount Seymour, and Golden Ears Provincial Parks. A treetop bird which is easy to hear but hard to see. In migration, especially in spring, also seen easily in lowland wooded areas like Queen Elizabeth Park, Stanley Park, and Point Roberts.

MacGillivray's Warbler

Fairly common in summer (late Apr. to late Sept.). It prefers dense shrubbery at all altitudes, sometimes in forest, but more often along streams, powerline rights-of-way, and avalanche slopes. Very common on the Squamish Highway north of Horseshoe Bay. Other good spots include Cypress, Mount Seymour, and Golden Ears Provincial Parks, Pitt Meadows, Pacific Spirit Regional Park, Point Roberts, and Campbell Valley Regional Park.

Black-headed Grosbeak

Fairly common summer (early May to early Sept.). Prefers deciduous forest at low altitudes, especially stands of black cottonwood and red alder. Easily overlooked because of its Robin-like song and retiring habits (usually staying within forest canopy). Good spots include Pitt Meadows, Minnekhada Regional Park, forest along the Coquitlam River, Burnaby Lake Regional Park, Pacific Spirit Regional Park, Ladner Harbour Park, Deas Island Regional Park, Point Roberts, and Campbell Valley Regional Park.

Lazuli Bunting

Rare in summer (mid-May to early Sept.). Prefers open, brushy areas. The most consistent spot has been the abandoned dump site on Premier Street in North Vancouver, now overgrown with grasses and brush patches. May be found, with luck, in Pitt Meadows, Colony Farm (Port Coquitlam), or woodlot edges and brushy areas in Surrey and Langley, but has an unhelpful tendency to turn up in a different spot every year.

American Tree Sparrow

Rare in summer (late Oct. to early Apr.), usually found in weedy fields and hedgerows in the Fraser Delta. Most often seen singly or in small flocks of up to 6 birds. Best places include Sea and Iona Islands, Westham Island, Brunswick Point, Boundary Bay Regional Park (south of Beach Grove), and the vicinity of the Boundary Bay airport.

Lapland Longspur

Uncommon transient, rare in winter (seen mainly from mid-Sept. to early May). This bird likes open fields, dikes, and jetties, often along shorelines; usually in flocks of 5 to 20 birds. Seen most often in late Sept. and Oct. Best places include Jericho Park, Iona Island (especially the south jetty), Brunswick Point and Roberts Bank, Boundary Bay dikes and the area around the Boundary Bay airport, and Blackie Spit.

Snow Bunting

Uncommon in winter (mid-Oct. to early Apr.). Found in many of the same places as Lapland Longspurs, sometimes in mixed flocks with them, but more likely to be seen in mid-winter. Particularly fond of jetties and shorelines. The two best localities are the Iona Island south jetty and the Tsawwassen jetty. Other likely spots include Brunswick Point, the Roberts Bank jetty, dikes around Boundary Bay, and Blackie Spit.

Yellow-headed Blackbird

Uncommon in summer (mainly mid-Apr. to mid-Sept.), rare in winter. The only breeding colony in the area, in a small freshwater marsh on Sea Island, is scheduled to be destroyed by airport expansion in 1993. However, this species is seen regularly also on Iona Island, Reifel Bird Sanctuary, Jericho Park, and Burnaby Lake, and may begin nesting regularly at one or more of these spots if suitable marsh habitat is provided.

Northern Oriole Uncommon in summer (early May to early Sept.). This bird has been increasing in numbers for the last 20 years, although it is still rather uncommon. It prefers large trees (especially cottonwoods or Lombardy poplars) in open areas. Local birds tend to be inconspicuous and to sing infrequently; orioles are more numerous than generally believed. Good spots to find them include Ladner Harbour Park, Deas Island Park, Blackie Spit (tall trees near base of the spit), golf courses on Lulu Island, and Pitt Meadows.

Rosy Finch Rare in winter (mainly Oct. to Apr.), and irregular and unpredictable in occurrence. Your best chance of finding this bird is to hike the trails above 1000 m altitude in Mount Seymour Provincial Park and Cypress Provincial Park (e.g. the Howe Sound Crest Trail) in late Oct. and Nov., before snow becomes too deep for hiking; they occur with some regularity in the North Shore Mountains in late fall. Lowland occurrences are usually within a day or two after heavy snowfalls in the mountains; it may be worth driving up the access roads to Cypress and Mount Seymour Parks, or checking the Stanley Park seawall or Pitt Lake dike for Rosy Finches, but you will be very lucky to find them outside the mountains.

Pine Grosbeak Casual in summer, rare in winter (mainly late Oct. to late Mar.). Like the preceding species, found mainly in the North Shore Mountains, but there are occasional records in "irruption years" in places like Point Roberts, Pitt Meadows, and the Point Grey Golf Course in Vancouver. However, the only place and time when you have a significant chance of finding this bird is in Cypress or Mount Seymour Parks in late Oct. or Nov.

Bibliography

Butler, R.W. and R. W. Campbell. 1987. *The Birds of the Fraser River Delta: Populations, Ecology, and International Significance.* Occasional Paper No. 65. Environment Canada, Canadian Wildlife Service, Ottawa.

Campbell, R.W., Shephard, M.G. and W. Weber. 1972. *Vancouver Birds in 1971.* Vancouver Natural History Society. Vancouver.

Campbell, R.W., Shephard, M.G. and R.H. Dent. 1972. *Status of Birds in the Vancouver Area in 1970.* Syesis 5:137-167.

Campbell, R.W., Shephard, M.G., Macdonald, B. and W. Weber. 1973. *Vancouver Birds in 1972.* Vancouver Natural History Society. Vancouver.

Campbell, R.W. et al. 1990. *The Birds of British Columbia.* Vol. 1 (loons through waterfowl) and Vol. 2 (diurnal birds of prey through woodpeckers). Canadian Wildlife Service, Royal British Columbia Museum, Victoria.

Campbell, R.W. et al. 1979. *Bibliography of British Columbia Ornithology,* Vols. 1 and 2. Royal British Columbia Museum, Victoria. (Note: Contains many references to papers and reports on Vancouver Checklist Area birds).

Grass, A. 1989. *The Birds of Golden Ears Provincial Park.* South Coast Region, BC Parks, North Vancouver.

Mark, D.M. 1984. *Where to Find Birds in British Columbia.* 2nd Edition. Kestrel Press, New Westminster.

Rodgers, J. 1974. *The Birds of Vancouver.* Bryan Publications, Vancouver.

Smith, K. et al. 1988. *Nature West Coast.* Sono Nis Press, Victoria. (Note: Has a useful "Migration Calendar").

Vancouver Natural History Society. 1988. *The Natural History of Stanley Park.* Schaefer, V. and A. Chen, eds. Vancouver.

Weber, W. et al. 1990. *Checklist of Vancouver Birds.* Vancouver Natural History Society. (Note: Gives abundance and seasonal status).

I N D E X   of Bird Species

Notes